CW00644669

THE BOYS WHO CYCLED EUROPE

ALEX PAVITT

The Boys Who Cycled Europe

Copyright © Alex Pavitt 2014

All rights reserved. No part of this publication may be reproduced, stored in a retrieval system, or transmitted in any form or by any means, electronic, mechanical, photocopying, recording or otherwise, without the prior permission of the author.

This book is sold subject to the condition that it shall not, by way of trade or otherwise, be lent, re-sold, hired out or otherwise circulated without the author's prior consent in any form of binding or cover other than that in which it is published and without a similar condition being included and this condition being imposed on the subsequent purchaser.

All photographs © Alex Pavitt

www.alexscycle.org

ISBN 13: 978-1-291-57727-3 (Print edition)
ISBN 13: 978-1-291-80029-6 (eBook edition)

For Tom

Introduction

Suddenly the sun peaked over the hills ahead of us and we were doused in the rich warmth. The heavy dew began to evaporate from the straw fields around us, forming a thick mist which drifted over the road. We were flying. Fuelled with excitement that today, after everything that had gone wrong we would finally make it. It was a feeling of pure euphoria. We were going to do it.

Gradually we left the pastures of Northern France behind and slowly our surroundings turned from green to grey. The sun was creeping up and so was the traffic. On any normal day it would have felt very dangerous with this amount of cars hurtling past us. However this was not a normal day. This was the final day. After this the cycling would be over. We could not stop grinning. All of our hard work was about to pay off. Soon we hit the suburbs of Paris. With the little boulangeries calling to us it was hard to resist temptation. However we decided we would wait until we reached our goal. Naturally our destination was *Le Tour Eiffel*. However we had factored in one stop, to drop off our panniers at the hostel. Somehow we had managed to navigate our way successfully from Manchester to Paris using just a few pieces of A4 paper. When the time came to take off our panniers we were already in the heart of Paris, our final city. We almost didn't care about making it to the

Eiffel Tower in our heads we had already completed our journey.

Nevertheless we mounted our bicycles for one last time in search of our goal. It's amazing what losing fifteen kilograms does to the feel of a bike. Despite the shaky start, getting used to the weightlessness, we were fast. We zoomed around the streets celebrating our success. We had no idea where we were going so eventually, after an hour of pedalling around the cobbles of the Champs Eilleyses, we somehow appeared at the base of the tower.

The sun was high in the sky by now, it was a wondrously sunny August day in Paris. Pedalling carefully through the hoards of tourists we found our way to a nice spot where we could have our victory photographed. Now it was over. High time to nurse ourselves into a food coma, feasting on our success.

I can still remember vividly that feeling, pure content. It was my first cycle tour and indeed the first time I had ever cycled further than 30 miles in a day. Despite cycling from a young age I have never been a big cyclist. I always enjoyed going out on small rides but rowing was always my first passion. It was at rowing where the idea of going on a cycle tour first began. Tom, Charles, and I were relaxing in the lounge on the sofas after a hard session. We had just finished our GCSE's and were all looking forward to the long summer we had ahead, as it was only June. We joked about how it would be good to go on holiday together, somewhere along the line Paris got suggested, and then later cycling. It was as simple as that. We said it initially as a joke, "Why don't we cycle to Paris, that would be even cheaper than getting the train". However that idea grew in my head, how hard could it be?

Somehow, after not much planning at all, by early August we were all ready to set off. We simply used Google maps to sort out a route. So off we went, armed with a few paper printouts, into the world of cycle touring.

Now with us having no training whatsoever the first day, of which we rode 100 kilometres, was awfully difficult. The tiredness combined with the torrential rainfall was really not pleasant. However it also left me feeling free. Something I had not experienced before with other holidays. We could go wherever we wanted, just as long as our legs could pedal us there. What if we didn't stop at Paris and kept going? When you're only expenditure is food and you are buying it cheaply, cycle touring is an extremely sustainable way of travelling. We were not using trains or planes with their large emissions to get to our destination. We were using our legs, although Charles often let loose large emissions in the tent which resulted in Tom and I evacuating!

Despite the first day we were graced with sunshine for every single day of our cycle and it was glorious. We were three lads out on an adventure. However it wasn't all plain sailing. Charles lost his wallet on the first day and he then left his phone on the ferry. Also as we were cycling onto the ferry at Dover we got hit by a sudden crosswind which resulted in us almost losing Tom overboard. Fortunately he managed to save himself. However his bike 'Julie' took the brunt of it. She had a bent rear wheel and a broken pannier rack. We also all had our fair share of punctures.

Somehow though, upon returning, I just wanted to go again. It was a holiday like no other, it tested my teamwork and decision making skills. The cycle left me with a buzz. I just had to do another one, a longer one. Fortunately Tom felt exactly the same. So a few weeks after returning from Paris we began drafting ideas for our next big cycling adventure.

We wanted to do something bigger and better than our Paris cycle. We wanted to be prepared, so we could cycle 160 kilometres in a day. This would require more fitness so we began cycling to rowing, a 30 kilometre round trip, building up our fitness on the bike.

Initially we toyed with the idea of continuing our cycle, beginning in Paris where we had ended previously. From there we could cycle to Portugal or further east towards Istanbul. We researched on blogs and gained inspiration from reading books. All the while solidifying in our minds that we were going to do something 'epic'. We thought about America, however that seemed too far away for two seventeen year old boys. We thought it would require too much logistical planning for transporting our bicycles. We therefore honed in on Europe. Right on our doorstep. Thus the idea of Tour d'Europe began. How far around Europe could we get on a low budget? We thought pretty far. We got out a map and began plotting points of places we wanted to go. After a few attempts we were able to draw a line through these points. There we had it, our route was more-or-less complete. We would begin in Northern Spain then wiggle our way into France, across the Pyrenees to the Mediterranean, from there we would go along to Saintes-Maries-De-La-Mer; then Nice and Monaco. After Monaco we would enter Italy, where we would finally turn North and head up to Turin, then across into Switzerland. After passing through Geneva we would begin the final push up to the Netherlands, where we would get a ferry back to Hull. Overall it would be a little over 3000 kilometres and take us through eight countries. As we would have to return in time to watch the Olympic rowing we would only have four weeks to cover this distance. It would certainly be a challenge; we could not wait.

The cycle to Paris was not the first long adventure that Tom and I had gone on. Our first major expedition was two years prior when we were just fifteen. We trekked 300 kilometres across the Sahara desert, in Morocco, over two weeks. This was my first proper experience of a true adventure. A fortnight sleeping under the stars, encased by sand dunes, many miles away from the nearest civilisation. It was wonderful, well it was until we all became terribly ill; you name the orifice we had things coming out of it. We all lost over a stone in body weight over those few days. We thought we were going to die in the desert. It was a hard time, and a harder task to go on to complete the trek whilst still recovering from the illness. Others had been transported to hospital but we carried on walking. In hindsight, it was that journey which kick-started my hunger and passion for adventures.

During the Desert Trek, like the Paris cycle, Tom and I raised money for the 'When You Wish Upon A Star' charity. A charity dedicated to making children with terminal illnesses wish's come true. From a young age I have raised money for charity. It is an easy thing to do, using your strengths to benefit others. The way I see it if you can help raise some important funds whilst doing something you enjoy then it really is a win-win. Our 'Europe Cycle' would be a level higher than anything either of us had tried to complete before. We would be totally on our own with no back up; no support vehicle. I therefore saw it as a great opportunity to raise a good amount of money for charity.

The MS Society is the UK's leading charity for multiple sclerosis. Its' main aims are to beat MS and they go about this by funding key research projects and providing support and assistance to those that are affected by MS. There are over 100,000 people in the UK living with MS thus making it one of the major illnesses in our country. It is for all these reasons why Tom and I thought it would be right and fitting to raise money for this very good cause. Like on our Paris cycle we decided to use 'Just Giving' to help facilitate donations, meaning people from all over the world could donate and see how they were supporting us reach our goal. We had the idea of posting updates every day onto our page so that people could follow our journey around Europe, and so that our mums would be reassured that we were still alive.

This year we would not be setting out on our first bicycle tour. This was important; it meant that hopefully we could learn from the mistakes we made last time. The biggest one by a mile would be not using print-outs from Google Maps. Although we made it to Paris it was not without its difficulties and for a 3000 kilometre journey that would be a lot of paper to print out! Instead I decided to invest in a small hand-held walking GPS. We could then use an online bicycle routing website to construct the route and then load it onto the GPS. All we would have to do then would be to follow the little line on the screen, oh and keep it stocked up with batteries. However that seemed a lot easier than heaving around hundreds of sheets of paper or carrying many different maps!

The biggest shock we had had when cycling to Paris was the sheer heaviness of our bikes, they were ridiculous. This was the main issue we wanted to address before setting off into Europe. How could we go lighter but without having to chop out toothbrushes in half? Our answer was to bivvy. If we each slept in a bivvy bag instead of a tent it would save a huge amount of weight. Bivvy bags are essentially waterproof covers for your sleeping bag. They pack up small and only weigh about half a kilo, exactly what we wanted. They would be perfect for what we planned to do as well, wild camp. We had read a lot about wild camping on the Internet and it seemed like such an amazing concept. In essence you camp where you want to. This means you have a free place to set up camp, saving money, and often in a more beautiful location. A location that you haven't taken a large detour to find, like you would with a traditional campsite.

It seemed perfect in everyway. Except things which sound too good to be true probably are. We had not ever experienced sleeping in bivvys, nor had we thought about insects, more importantly mosquitoes. The mosquitoes would have loved it if we had taken bivvy bags however unfortunately for them at the last moment we decided to stick to what we knew, please our parents, and take a light weight tent.

Slowly but surely we began to consolidate what we were going to take with us. Taking only the essential, as we would only have two panniers each. We sent our bikes in for one complete overhaul and service, a good idea too as my stem appeared to have broken! Until eventually our bikes and bags were ready. There was one slight problem though. One which was making me feel increasingly apprehensive about what we were about to undertake. With the pressures of our AS level exams and sorting out the bikes and gear. I had no time whatsoever to get out on my bike. Cycling to rowing had stopped and I had done zero kilometres for the past few months. Let alone anything with any amount of weight on my bike. Tom was the same however Tom has some sort of divine power that he always seems to stay fit and strong no matter how little exercise he does. I am quite different, a couple of months not on the bike meant I now felt very nervous about even going out for a couple of hours. I was worried that if I couldn't even complete two hours without any panniers then that would not put me in a positive mental state for cycling over 3000 kilometres around Europe in a weeks time. Damned if I do and damned if I don't. I was truly stuck between a rock and a hard place. Until eventually I decided enough was enough and I went out to see how far I could ride. They were fast miles, unlike what we would be doing for the real thing, however they felt good. They reassured me. I would just have to do my training with a fully laden bike on the actual adventure itself.

Sooner than expected, departure day loomed towards us. There certainly was no turning back now. I just wished to be out there and riding my bicycle. The suspense was killing me. The 'what if' questions were building inside my head with the ever-growing anticipation. A week today we would be in Spain. A week today we would be in France. Then before I knew it. It was time. I was packing up my panniers and loading them into the car, for the journey to the Portsmouth ferry. Our bikes, Julie and Samantha, were secured onto the bicycle rack. Just one sleep to go and then we would be on the ferry from Portsmouth to Bilbao and beginning our journey. Our charity page was set up and our target set at £3000, we were aiming to raise £1 per kilometre cycled. Buzzing with anticipation, Tom and I settled in for what was likely to be the worst night's sleep of our lives.

Journey to the Start
Manchester to Bilbao

It was a cloudy grey day, typical British summertime weather, however Tom and I didn't care because soon we would be in sunny Spain —or so we hoped. The drive from Manchester to Portsmouth was long and boring, although our route back to Manchester would hardly be direct and fast. Eventually we reached the ferry terminal and it was time to leave England. We unloaded the car and loaded up our bikes for the very first time. In hindsight it would have definitely been a good idea to get some practice in with a fully laden bike. These bikes were really heavy, made even heavier by the two huge carrier bags we had each, brimming with food for our ferry journey.

Our crossing would take over a day and we would arrive in Bilbao the following evening. Then we would have to find our hostel, which should be easy using our GPS, then after a good nights sleep the cycle would begin. That was our plan. I had gone over it countless times in my head but there was nothing more I could do now. Now we were venturing into the unknown, and most probably vastly underprepared.

The charity donation page was up and running and already we were receiving donations. This was partly helped by Ewan McGregor re-tweeting one of my tweets.

My mum had agreed to post updates of our travels onto the page for people to view and track our progress. Good luck texts were flying in constantly, making us smile and face up to the reality of what we were about to attempt. Just like that, all those months of preparation had finally come down to this. We were 17, exams were over, and we were now at the starting point. Walking along the edge of a cliff staring directly into the precipice. All we could do now was hope nothing would go wrong, however we knew from past experiences that that was unlikely to occur.

With everything ahead of us we bid farewell to my parents and jumped onto our bikes. We pushed off into the unknown. The bikes were unbearably heavy but luckily we only had to cycle about 300 metres before we stopped for passport control. They gave us our keys to access our room on board the ferry then we were free to join the long queue that is synonymous with ferry riding. Fortunately we were put into a motorcycle queue which was the first to board the boat. Not wanting to repeat what happened on the Paris cycle Tom and I decided it would be best to walk our bikes onto the ferry. Sure enough we managed to do it without bending a wheel or breaking a pannier rack, off to a successful start –long may it continue!

Once on board we began the lengthy process of unloading our bikes and securing them to the ferry. Once they were secure and we had put every conceivable lock we had around them it was time to load ourselves up. That involved carrying about five large bags each and blocking every single corridor in our quest to find our room. Eventually we found it and within about five minutes it was already a heap. Our room comprised of four beds, a desk, a small ensuite bathroom, and no windows. It was an odd sensation not having any windows, it made the room somewhat prison like. In fact I am sure some prison cells are nicer than the cabin we were staying in. This is because it seemed our bathroom fan was linked to all the other bathrooms around us. So whenever any of our neighbours wanted to relieve themselves we had the personal delight of having the smell of their business fill our cabin, not a pleasant experience.

Keen to leave the room (it was filling up with all sorts of smells which I wont go in to) we were in the mood to explore the ship. We also desperately needed to stretch our legs. We soon found our way to the top of the boat, the observation deck and tiny swimming pool which looked more the size of a hot tub, one key difference though the water was ice cold. As it was such a grey and dull day there wasn't a great deal to see so we decided to head back inside the ship. On our brief explore we had spied a sports bar, no doubt this would be where we would spend the majority of our time over the forthcoming hours, as they were screening both the Tour de France and Wimbledon.

Unsurprisingly we did stay there for a good few hours, all the while working our way through the mountains of food we had brought with us on board. Our thinking behind this was that we needed to 'carb load'. Although I am sure a large cheesecake doesn't really qualify as carbohydrate loading, it is better to be safe than sorry. The people around us were looking on in awe as we devoured almost a weeks worth of shopping in one big sitting.

Eventually we decided to call it a night. Our bellies had grown increasingly full and this had had the effect of making us quite sleepy. Just a little tip for people about to go on a 3000 kilometre cycle, don't overeat it always seems like a good idea but it definitely isn't. Suffice to say our stomachs were calling out when we eventually slumped down into our beds. We had decided to get a relatively early night and rest up for Sunday, our first proper day of cycling. Sunday would be a big test; we would be aiming for about 90-100 kilometres with our fully laden bikes.

We woke the next morning totally confused. Was it morning? We had no idea because of the lack of windows. Our room stayed the same level of darkness all day long. Unfortunately over eating the previous night had taken its toll on me, I was now feeling really ill. Not what you want when you are about to cycle around Europe.

We elected to have a lazy morning because we had nothing else to do. Oh, except go to a talk on the Whales in the Bay of Biscay however that wasn't either of our cups of tea, so we stayed in bed. We read our books, and Tom played some Pokémon on his Game Boy Advance, until we eventually roused at lunchtime. Our next big meal. We decided that we might as well eat as much of the food as possible because our Ferry would dock in the evening and we would spend most our time finding the hostel. Clearly we hadn't learnt from last night's exploits.

By the time we were once again feeling nicely brimmed with food we were also a little bit tired and restless. There was little to occupy us on the ferry and we still had a good few hours to kill. It was then when we were watching the sea go past the windows and the Tour de France was on the television when Tom posed the question.

"Do you think we should shave our legs?"

I mulled it over in my mind. We had nothing to do and all the professional cyclists had shaved legs —that's my justification.

"Why not," I replied.

And so it was. We began the process of shaving our legs. Allegedly if we had a crash it would now be much easier to clean and dress the wound. We would also have a slight aerodynamic advantage. However without any shaving foam it was a very slow process. We were relying on the shampoo dispenser in the shower to provide the foam we needed. We took turns, all the while laughing our heads off at how ridiculous we looked. Gradually our legs became bald and hairless. Eventually, a whole two hours after beginning, they were finished. We had not felt our legs like this since we were about twelve and it felt bizarre. I began with much hairier legs than Tom so felt very odd. Everything was suddenly very breezy, our legs felt exposed. However although we did slightly look more of the part of road cyclists now we both had a feeling that our manhood was in tatters. It was worth it though because I don't think either of us had ever laughed so much in our lives. A great way, if not slightly peculiar, to begin our adventure.

With that ordeal over with we had to begin the tedious job of tidying our room and packing of our bags because the ferry would shortly be arriving into Bilbao. It is amazing how messy a room can become in just a few hours! It was an odd feeling, our time on the ferry was almost over. Before we would know it we would be at the hostel and then beginning our cycle 3000 kilometres around Europe. Finally what we were trying to do was starting to sink in. This would be a huge undertaking. A month of cycling over 160 kilometres a day, with just a few rest days. Just me and Tom, boys cycling Europe. There would no doubt be some very hard times and decisions we would have to make, and there is no way to prepare. We would have to adjust to life on the road. In just a couple of day's time we would be wild camping for the first time ever. In just an hours time we would be entering Spain a country neither of us could speak a word of its language. A lot to adjust to, a lot to learn, and a lot to face; I was only just realising all this.

Packing up all our stuff took less time than expected and before we knew it we were in our Lycra, panniers packed, and food eaten, ready to cycle. One slight problem, the boat was still to dock. No problem though we would just continue to watch the Tour de France, only now we felt the part with our shaved legs.

Finally it was time to depart the boat and boy were we glad to wave goodbye to the prison cell we had for our room, odd smells and all. We made our way down to the bottom car deck to find our bikes, Julie and Samantha, perched against the railings just where we had left them. Nothing looked broken or out of place. Success we had made it to Spain unscathed or without serious problem or so we thought, I'll let you be the judge of the girly shaved legs.

We loaded our panniers onto our bicycles I clipped in the Garmin GPS and when we were given the signal we began the ride out of the ferry. We emerged and straight away were bathed in the warm Spanish sunlight. It was glorious. This was how we envisaged it. Blue skies, shining sun, and smooth asphalt. We made our way to passport control who waved us through without checking our passports and we had officially made it. Now we had to cycle the 25 kilometres into Bilbao to the Hostel. I turned on the GPS, nothing. I turned it off and back on again, nothing. I took the batteries out and put them back in, switched it on, nothing. We had no maps. We were at a ferry port at the very beginning of our journey, we had cycled the grand total of 100 metres from Portsmouth and we now had no maps. All we had was a brown blank screen with our blue route etched onto it. No roads, nothing. We had no option but to cycle forwards and so we did. Somehow we would have to make our way to the centre of Bilbao following just a dot and making sure it stayed on a blue line. From there we would have to make a plan. Disaster!

Just when we thought everything was going swimmingly it all went disastrously wrong. We began pedalling tediously not wanting to take a wrong turn. In my head I just kept on going over what had happened, I just couldn't understand why the map wasn't showing up because it was working on the ferry. Something had happened to it and now its memory had been wiped. If we didn't find some maps in Bilbao we would be well and truly done in.

Eventually we reached the worst thing imaginable when you are navigating map-less in an unknown country. A road block. Not just the road block with a few builders that you get in the UK but this one had a Policeman who instructed us to turn around and go back. Unfortunately he only spoke minor English, "No cycle," this was illustrated with a finger point back the way we came. Back towards the ferry? We were very confused. The only turning so far had been for the motorway and we definitely didn't want to cycle along that. We tried to explain that we had to carry on. He then seemed confused himself and went back inside his hut. We were very confused and did not want to go back, as the policeman seemed a little bored of us now we decided to just go for it. When he turned his back we did a short sharp burst around the roadblock and sped down the road, we were out of sight within seconds. Luckily for us he either did not see or did not want to give chase.

We were now cycling in what appeared to be a large industrial estate. Only one thing was odd, it was eerily quiet. No one was about, no cars, no trucks, nothing. It was the type of place you see in movies where people are brought by murdering psychopaths to be killed. This combined with the police roadblock seemed very odd. Where on earth were we? We decided the best option would be to increase our speed and carry on creeping down the blue line on the GPS, hopefully towards Bilbao.

Eventually we emerged by a river in a much more built up area of the city. This was good we thought, things were finally taking a turn for the better. That was until we came to cross the river. There was a large rowing event on, this meant the bridge which we wanted to use to cross was lifted up and out of the way making it impossible for us to cross the river. Tom and I both being keen rowers enjoyed watching the rowing for a short while, waiting for the bridge to come down. However eventually we conceded, we would have to find another way to cross the river. We cycled for miles down the river, battling strong winds, before we finally found a place to cross. Even this involved heaving our heavy bikes up about fifty steps. It turned out that without a map we were doing a nice little tour of Bilbao, the football stadium, the Guggenheim art museum, until finally, many hours after setting off from the ferry, we reached our hostel. Purely by dumb luck we had arrived. Success!

Unfortunately not. Somehow I had been a complete idiot and booked the hostel for a month earlier. Our reservation was meaningless. Not only that but they only had one bed available. This day really wasn't turning out to be the relaxed easy start we had dreamt about all those times. We were in Bilbao, homeless, and map-less. Could it really be much worse?

Thankfully the wonderful guy on reception rang up another nearby hostel which happened to have beds free. He also gave us a map of Bilbao so we had directions to the hostel. Finally a map! We thanked him and set off towards 'Surfers Hostel', not really knowing what to expect. All we knew was that there would be two beds with our names on them!

A short ten minute ride and we had made it. This time for good. Our home for the night. It also turned out to be pretty cheap and fantastically clean. We had somehow hit the jackpot. We unloaded our bikes and collapsed back onto our beds, the torments of the day weighing us down. If all that had happened on a 25 kilometre day who knows what would happen on a full day of cycling? Let alone we still had the problem of no map of Europe. I set about thinking of what to do. We would just have to find a petrol station in the morning I thought and buy a map of Northern Spain and gradually make up a route again. I say petrol station because tomorrow would be Sunday so they would be the only shops open. However I vowed to give the GPS one last effort. I played with the settings, to no avail. I was just about to give up all hope till Tom suggested taking out its memory card and giving it a wipe. Doubtfully I removed it, wiped the gold connectors with my thumb and inserted it back into the device with a push of my finger. Then as if by magic it whirred into life. Suddenly in my hand I had maps for the entirety of Europe. Everything was not lost! Maybe by some stroke of luck we might make it around Europe after all.

The simple act of wiping a memory card had instilled life in our weary bodies. I was still fighting off a cold but now we felt ready. We were ready to begin our journey. I received a text from my mum informing us that we had already raised over £1000 for the MS Society and that raised our spirits even higher. This was just the beginning and somehow an initially dreadful day had turned amazing. Tomorrow the test of the cycling would reign in and our adventure around Europe would commence.

It Can Only Get Easier
Cycling Day 1
Bilbao to Mutriku

At 6:30 my alarm went off. I was already awake though, excited to finally start this mammoth journey. I quickly turned my phone off, carefully, making sure not to wake up anyone else in the dorm. I then rolled over to nudge Tom awake. Finally after a good few minutes of prodding he rose from his deep stupor.

It was time to get ready and go. However this was made increasingly difficult by the amount of people sleeping in the hostel and the fact everyone was fast asleep. It was a Sunday after all. We tip-toed around the hard wooden floors; making hundreds of trips from bed to bike, carrying just a couple of items at a time. It was a very inefficient system of bike packing I must admit. We then went about filling water-bottles, and using the toilet one last time before heading into the unknown.

When it finally came time to leave at about 7:20 still nobody was awake. As we were ready and raring we decided to just go for it and leave, without officially checking out. Carefully unlocking the front door of the hostel we pushed our bikes out on to the cobbles of the San Pedro Plaza. We clipped in and were off.

It was a very unceremonious start to our journey, no well wishers, no family, just a few pigeons hanging around looking for some left over breakfast –they were sorely disappointed.

"Now, which way?"

Tom was looking at me eagerly. I pointed down the road and off we went. Minutes later I realised my mistake; we retreated and went the other way. Getting out of Bilbao proved much more difficult than I had anticipated. Our once prompt an early start to the day slowly whittled away as we found ourselves lost down the many lovely side streets Bilbao has to offer. Fortunately our luck took a turn for the better, as I became more proficient with the GPS; we found our way to Zabaloexte and out of Bilbao.

The weather was perfect. A lovely 24°C, sunny and the best part it wasn't windy. Once we found our way we covered those first few kilometres very fast. It was lovely. Very few cars about, as it was a Sunday, although there were plenty of cyclists. What could be better? The initial feeling of excitement was still present although my cold had taken a turn for the worse. I was very bunged up and coughing every other second. It was horrible. It didn't make for the most enjoyable cycling; the cycling didn't make for the most enjoyable cold, although I don't think I have ever described a cold as enjoyable before.

I was amazed at how empty everywhere was. Bilbao is a major city in northern Spain with almost one million inhabitants. Yet we had only seen about 10 people so far in the morning.

After almost an hour of pedalling we were safely off the main roads and out of the Bilbao suburbs. We took a short stop to put on some sun cream –now it was feeling like a summer holiday, minus my cold. We had decided to start the trip with an easier day rather than go straight for 100 miler days. Our aim for today was the town Mutriku. It was almost 100 kilometres away on our route so we thought this was a good target. It also looked like a decent town on the maps so we thought we would be able to pick up some food there. However getting there was about to get very difficult.

We had hit the hills. Almost simultaneously as we entered the countryside of the Basque region the roads started to undulate beneath our wheels. Our legs were getting a proper test for the mountainous stretches that lay ahead. I kept thinking to myself, 'Why didn't I do more practice with a fully laden bike, rather why didn't I do *any* practice with a fully laden bike?' It was hard going, made harder by the demoralising sight of a group of old Spanish men on their racing bikes tear past us on an uphill. We shall never live it down. My legs were on fire. My throat was aching. I could barely breathe because of my blocked nose. It was no longer fun. One hour into a 3000 kilometre cycle round Europe and I was already ready for the finish. This is not going good I thought to myself.

I felt like a fraud. So much planning had gone into this trip. All the sponsorship money for the MS Society, it would all be for nothing. I found it hard facing the realisation that I probably wouldn't be able to complete this journey, then I felt instantaneous guilt because then I would ruin it for Tom as well. We were a team, this couldn't happen could it? I wished I could have gone back in time and done more practice and preparation. However no amount of preparation I think could have prepared me for the real thing, with the flu.

Tom sensed something was up. However I could not bring myself to tell him how terrible I was feeling. I decided I would push through, make it through the day, and see how I felt tomorrow.

As I decided this, like a miracle, we cycled past our first open shop of the day, hallelujah! It was a petrol station; it had a large array of fresh bread and some very questionable looking sandwiches. Tom was adventurous and selected a sandwich, which we still have no idea what it contained as neither of us speak Spanish. I, not wanting to upset my stomach further, opted for some bread, sweets and fruit juice to get some vitamin C in me.

Sitting down outside the shop watching a trail of ants ferry crumbs to and fro I knew I had gone one too far. The fruit juice was a bad idea. I felt it coming, so jumped up and ran around the back of the shop where I emptied the contents of my stomach. Need I say, it was not pleasant. Although I did feel slightly better afterwards I now had no food inside me and we still had 60 kilometres left to cycle. My fever was mounting too. Tom was great, he understood I needed help and offered to carry the tent to lighten my bike load as I was feeling so weak. This helped a lot. So we pushed off and headed into the mountains, for a cool breeze.

The next few kilometres were really tough. The roads increased in gradient and we continued to rise in elevation.

Yet still it seemed the whole of Spain was asleep, apart from the cyclists because we had seen plenty of them. Although I did feel terrible, I found it hard to ignore the beauty of the scenery around us. The smooth tarmac offered a stark contrast to the luscious pine trees and vivid green shrubbery. We curved our way through forests and up long tiresome hills totally immersed in a different world away from civilisation. It was sublime.

Then like that, we turned a corner. The road sharply rose; it must've been 10 percent, which doesn't sound too bad except we could not see the end of the road. It just kept rising and rising. We were now at an elevation of over 300 metres and had already climbed over a kilometre in ascent. Our initial idea of easing ourselves into this mammoth journey had crashed and burned. This was going to be a hard day after all.

Just after twelve we were totally fatigued and needed a rest, as we had only had one break and that was for breakfast. We were nearing the summit of the hill and about 350 metres above sea level; the road had given way to a small lay-by in which was some logs. Time for lunch. By now my appetite had almost recovered, about time too after 60 kilometres on an empty stomach! However although I was hungry my stomach would only let me eat in small manageable bits, eventually though I finished my loaf of bread. Tom had eaten his questionable sandwiches in about two bites and was now opening about a kilogram of chocolate. He looked pretty tired too so it was probably a good idea he was eating so much. I had already burnt over 4000 calories so was definitely running in deficit. I tried not to dwell on this and focused on how far left there was to Mutriku, we were going to make it, we had to make it.

After lunch about 200 metres further up the road my rear tyre totally deflated. Disaster. I had been dreading this occurring from before we set off, the worst thing to happen whilst cycling are punctures. They occur out of the blue, stop you in your tracks and then require time and effort to fix before you can set off again. We pulled over and set about fixing my back tyre. This was made increasingly difficult because the big tyre I had fitted before we set off was nigh impossible to put back on once I had fitted a new inner tube. After almost an hour of willing it into place we got it back in and the wheel on, Phew. It turned out I had not got a puncture but had just over inflated the tyre the night before at the hostel, the pressure had built up in the heat of the day and finally the valve had let the air out. However the most worrying thing to happen we only realised upon setting off again.

My rear brake calliper had totally seized up and would now not work. No amount of lube or anything would allow it to work. It was completely knackered. Just what I wanted on day one of a 3000 kilometre cycle, especially when it had only been serviced the week before.

As always we mustered on; my bike maintenance course had helped me so I disconnected my rear brake and we set off to do the last 20 kilometres in to Mutriku.

Finally some downhills, our morning efforts were paying off as we were rewarded with stunning sweeping descents through costal towns on the Bay of Biscay. It was so lovely and soon we found ourselves in the town of

Ondarroa. It was a classic Spanish costal town and very pretty. We knew we would have to find some food to eat as we had nothing. The only problem was we had only seen one shop open all day —the petrol station earlier. As this seemed like a decent sized town we thought surely there must be some open places, it is the summer holidays after all! However after a lot of searching and getting lost down tiny side streets we couldn't find anything but bars. So we asked a lovely old woman and she pointed us to a kebab vendor. What a result, I had never had a kebab before but I sure was looking forward to this. We decided to keep them for dinner, as although we were hungry we weren't sure whether we would find any more food. Then yet again we got a stroke of luck as we were leaving Ondarroa when we saw an open shop. It was called 'Alimentacion', -which means food- result! Tom went in while I stayed with the bikes and after about 20 minutes he came out, looking like he had just done the weekly shop. With about three carrier bags and a five-litre bottle of water.

"Oh my god, how are we going to be able to carry all this?" I asked, amazed at how much he had bought. However he had come up trumps the food both dried and fresh looked great and was really cheap. Somehow, I am still not quite sure how we managed to fix all the food and drink onto our bikes even using hundreds of bungee cords. Our once speedy racing bikes were now looking like trans-Saharan camels loaded up with all our treasures. We quickly ate our Kebabs —which were divine- and covered the last 5 kilometres to Mutriku.

They were hard kilometres, bikes fully laden and feeling ill. However we made it! Our goal for the day had been met. Now we had to find somewhere to set up camp.

Neither of us had ever rough camped before. We decided it would be a good idea to do it on our Europe cycle because we had read so many peoples blogs saying how amazing it is. Also it is more hardcore. Without ever doing it before that did make us very apprehensive about choosing our very first spot. It also didn't help that we were in a foreign country so if we were discovered during the night, chances were we would not be able to explain ourselves. All this made me very nervous about the idea. We knew what we were looking for however in hilly costal towns we found it hard to find a place where we would be invisible and not cause a disturbance. After a few stops and checking out areas I spotted a footpath sign leading up a hill and suggested we check it out. Tom held the bikes while I went up and had a look, the settings looked perfect there were plenty of trees to provide cover however I couldn't see an area big enough to put a tent. On my walk back down the hill a saw a little track leading off to the side I followed it and saw it opened up into a clearing of grass. This was totally out of sight and just what we had been looking for. What were the chances of that? We had struck lucky again. Running back down the hill I told the good news to Tom. Finally we could relax.

Once we had the tent up we made noodles and soup with the food Tom had got. It was probably a bad idea eating this in hindsight. I immediately felt really ill and proceeded to throw up thick dark blood along with my kebab, it was horrible. I felt really weak. So I decided to have a nap while Tom ventured down to the beach for a swim. Then they started.

WOOF, WOOF, WOOF, the dogs began. The barking would never stop. They were in some kennels at the bottom of the clearing and could see us. The smell of dinner must have alerted them to our presence. What a mistake that was. We tried everything, ignoring them, shouting at them moving away, they just would not stop. This was going to be a fun nights sleep...

Time to Die
Cycling Day 2
Mutriku to Saint-Jean-de-Luz

It was a bad night's sleep. With Toms snoring and the consistent unrelenting dog barks I didn't manage to have much rest. I had not slept in a tent in a good few months and it showed, despite my extreme tiredness and fatigue I found it nigh impossible to drift off.

Eventually, after a night of lying down feeling sorry for myself, the dreaded sound of the alarm woke me from my daze. Tom roused, raring for another day in the saddle. I was just glad we would be leaving the dogs. I am normally a dog person. I used to have a lovely big Golden Retriever when I was younger called Cherry, she was the best dog a small boy could ask for. Cherry would never bark and despite her size was a big softie. I imagined most dogs would be like her, no they're not. That one nights experience has put me off having a dog ever again. It was not a night I would like to repeat anytime soon.

After putting our sleeping bags away and dressing ourselves we finally made it out of the tent. "Brrrr", It was cold. The cloudy weather totally summed up my feelings, overcast and glum. We slowly and laboriously went about the process of putting the tent away for the first time. Somehow I just couldn't stomach it and immediately threw up over a nearby bush. 'Oh please let this be the last of it,' I remember wishfully thinking to myself. It wasn't. The day started on a low; I felt worse than the afternoon before.

Not being able to stomach any breakfast I would have to start cycling with an empty stomach again. This was bad because I couldn't afford to lose weight this early in the trip; I still had nearly 3000 kilometres and a month left to cycle who knows what might happen between now and then? It was a very slow and dreary start to the day. It was the first time we had packed up camp, so it took us a while packing the bikes and transporting them down to the road. Finally an hour and a half after the alarm going off it was time to bid farewell to the dogs −a moment I cherish to this day. Making sure that we had left no signs of a camping ground we set off on day two.

Within a few metres it was clear Tom's legs were still tired from the day before as well, we had climbed over 2000 metres in ascent. However he was in a much better state than I was. We decided before we set off that day that we would pedal on slowly and see how we felt. It was too early in our trip to take one of our scheduled days off. We only had four scheduled and what if something unforeseen happened in the coming weeks, then we would not be able to complete it. So we decided a few kilometres would be better than none. Our original target was to make it across the border and into France, where at least we would be able to speak to people. Though that morning a more realistic target seemed the 50 kilometres to San Sebastian. I knew Tom wanted to push further than this. He was and has always been very good at just pushing through the pain. As much as I wanted to do this, I was worried about the consequences, I felt I would rather have a lighter day and try to recover a little. We agreed that we were definitely getting as far as San Sebastian and would re-assess the situation there. That was our plan.

Right from the start we had a stroke of luck. Rather than a five kilometre detour round an estuary at Deba we were able to walk our bikes across a foot bridge. It was a better start to the cycling than the previous day where we just got lost. The cycling was the best of the trip those first few kilometres; we averaged almost 30kph, thanks to a sweet tailwind and wondrously flat costal roads. We cycled through lovely little villages nestled into the hillside, through small arched tunnels through the cliffs. Lovely cobbled streets, we cycled past not on, they are always nicer to look at than to travel on. It was really beautiful. The once misty and foggy morning had opened up into a bright day of blue skies with fluffy cotton like clouds.

We were making such fast miles it looked like we were going to make San Sebastian by 10:30 without much effort. It is amazing how a bicycle can make you feel better. We stopped in Getaria, which is a lovely old Basque town with a large catholic church in the centre. It had a long deserted sandy beach and we posed while a confused looking Spaniard took some photos of us next to it.

Again we were so surprised about the huge number of Spaniards out on their bicycles. Not only that they all were riding really expensive bikes worth well over £3000! So much for Spain being in billions of debt and having the largest unemployment in Europe. From what we saw they all lived very affluent lives in the north. I always enjoy seeing other cyclists out on the road. I find it reaffirms what I am doing and it is nice to have someone to share your time with even if it is only for a few minutes. That was what was great about going cycling with Tom. We were not alone, we could always joke around; we had someone going through the same things we were going through. An experience shared is an experience gained. I was also beginning to appreciate how important it is to have someone there when I was feeling low. Tom never ceased to brighten the mood. He always had a smile on his face, no matter how much he was hurting. I found this deeply reassuring and I think it made us work well as a team. I was the thinker and the navigator, Tom made sure we stayed a team and was the motivator. Together we were going to conquer Europe by bicycle.

The roads were still going downhill as we turned towards the coast again. We were now just a few kilometres from San Sebastian. We were on course to make it to France. I was recovering; my legs and cold seemed much better when I was on the bike. The cycling was distracting me, focusing my mind elsewhere, which was good. However after a few large roundabouts I couldn't help but notice the road which we had been following had become distinctly more major. We had decided during the planning that we would follow bigger roads, as they are generally more direct. However we didn't mean to travel on many dual carriageways. It soon became apparent that this was no small dual carriageway.

We had been following the N-634 and river Oria all morning when suddenly as we neared San Sebastian it merged into the GI-20. This was bad news. The GI-20 is a major road which acts as a feeder from the motorway A8. In other words all the motorway traffic which is travelling to San Sebastian, which is most, travels on this road. This makes it the equivalent of a motorway. Not the best cycling road I can tell you now. The problem was when we merged onto it we had no idea what we were in store for. Four lanes in each direction of hell. Cars and trucks hurtling down as the speed limit was 90kph. The orchestra of horns began. Irate drivers were shouting at us as they sped past. Cars screeching on their brakes as they passed us far too close. We were going to die. In the next 20 minutes I forgot about the whole trip, my cold, everything. We had to get off the road before we were killed. The road had other ideas. With no junctions off we had no option but to carry on. This was bad; we shouldn't have been there, this was apparent by the fuming looks of drivers as they saw us pedalling as fast as we could with fully laden bikes. We were pedalling for freedom. We were pedalling for our lives. We were granted neither. Eventually the hard shoulder opened up so I shouted to Tom and we stopped in it. I could feel my heart beating through my chest; I had literally just brushed a car moments earlier. We looked at our route. Now was not the time to question why we had used this road. Now was the time to find out how we could get off. Tom was as shaken up as I was. There was a junction in about three kilometres or the junction we were meant to take in about seven. Tom wanted to go the whole seven but I convinced him that the junction in three kilometres would be a better option. We could work out a new route from there.

That was it. Just three kilometres left and we would be free. The worst ten minutes of my life. Just before we set off I decided to switch on my rear light and we put on our fluorescent jackets just to help be seen. What a good time for the batteries in my light to run out, 'fingers crossed there are no tunnels' I thought to myself. There were. As we rounded the bend from our stopping points we saw the signs telling us to check our lights for the tunnels. How on earth were we going to be able to make it alive? We were narrowly being missed as it was in the sunlight. If I wasn't before I really was now shitting it. Pardon my Spanish. We entered the unlit tunnel, using other car lights to guide our way. Luckily we could already see the other side. We sprinted. Pushed as fast as we could. It just wasn't fast enough. A huge HGV had crept up behind us only to realise there were two young cyclists in his way. He couldn't change lane. He could only go forward. Tom was in front of me, the HGV was right behind me. I could feel it ready to pounce, eat up my back wheel and me along with it. Then "SCREEEEEEEEEECH," The driver noticed us and slammed on his breaks. His wheels locked up. He began to skid. Everything suddenly began to play out in slow motion. Sweat dripped onto my handlebars from my brow. My legs pumped. My heart jumped out of my chest. My lungs strained for fresh air. My eyes dilated craving the sunlight. Then they were rewarded. We had made it through the tunnel.

We were still far from off the road. Although we had just escaped death by HGV we had not escaped death by GI-20 yet. Keeping up the momentum we had built up in the tunnel we sped down the road. The HGV driver had now moved out into the middle lane and came past us blaring his horn. I'm sure we had given each other heart attacks. Then like a miracle the sign of the junction came. Not a moment to soon. Those few minutes have without doubt taken years off my life. The day Tom and I almost got killed when we cycled on a motorway. Once off that death trap Tom agreed with me that it was a good decision to get off while we were still alive. However the problem we faced now was that we were lost, without maps in Spain and somehow we had to find our way to the French border. This was about 30 kilometres east and we could only use a little Garmin GPS to guide us there.

I hesitated programming the GPS to send us to the French border after the fiasco a few days earlier. We really couldn't afford to lose all our maps again. Eventually I decided to just go for it. I clicked where we wanted ago and after a short while a cycle-able route had been calculated. Everything was not lost. By this time it was almost lunch. As we were so close to San Sebastian we decided to take a little detour to see if we could find a shop that was open. You'd think that being a Monday everywhere would be open, they weren't. After a short while we came across a large supermarket which was open though and bought some lovely fresh baguettes and fruit juice. This time I managed to stomach it and keep it down. I was definitely improving. We both knew we were going to make it into France today and that was a good feeling. It felt as if we had conquered the start and were now truly immersed into our adventure.

The GPS proved to be an invaluable piece of equipment; it had saved our bacon on many occasions already. Not to mention it acted as our super accurate cycle computer. However its usability was very frustrating, it certainly took us around the houses when navigating us to the French border. It insisted on taking us down roads which didn't exist. Telling us to turn left where we no longer could. This proved very annoying. We ended up doing circles around one village about ten times, as we could not find the correct exit to take. After getting off our bikes and lifting them down some steps we found ourselves totally by chance on the right road. A lot of time was wasted and it wasn't until about 3pm when we made it to Irun, the last Spanish town. Tom was wishing we had now continued the extra four kilometres on the death road because more than likely we would have made it to France many hours earlier. I was content that we made it to the French border in one piece at least.

Finally after what had turned into a hard and stressful day, we cycled past all the border traffic and straight into country number two, France.

We decided that once across the border we would start to look for places to rough camp. I was looking for somewhere that was similar to our first spot, minus the dogs. We cycled down dirt tracks, roads off to the side and up hills but we found nothing. We were still too close to the border for open spaces of greenery. Eventually Tom thought he had spotted an ideal place on the opposite side of the road. He liked the look of it but when I checked the grass was almost up to my knees. I knew it was bad to camp in long grass and didn't want to disrupt the person's field by trampling it flat. I told this to Tom and reluctantly he agreed to carry on cycling, we would surely find something better.

The sky was now turning a deeper orange as the sun began to set. We still had nowhere to camp. We had even followed a few signs to campsites but given up after a few kilometres. Some travel advice; if a French sign says that something is two minutes away, it is probably almost a days cycle away. They forget to tell you it is only two minutes if you are doing just shy of the speed of light. We cycled on and on, till the border was a thing of the past and we were in fully-fledged France, still nothing. We pulled over and looked ahead; it didn't look like there were any possible spots for camping up ahead. We made the call 'next place we pass we will stop and ask for rooms.' We were going to have to go up market and stay in a hotel. Eventually, just after we had cycled through Saint-Jean-de-Luz, we noticed a hotel offering rooms for 60€. This was just what we were looking for. Basic and cheerful, it also looked really modern. We wheeled up our bikes to the entrance and with our most endearing smiles on approached the female receptionist. We were in luck; they had rooms available. She wanted to store our bikes out the back but we insisted and she kindly let us take them to our room which conveniently was on the ground floor.

We had made it, a night in a much-needed bed. We even got a large wall mounted TV so I knew what we'd be doing after we had got some food. Now that I was off the bike I had become very ill again. Coughing profusely and feeling really nauseous. I felt worse than the previous night. Hopefully a good nights rest in a proper bed would cure it. I was beginning to think we were the world's worst adventurers, ill, not being able to do a full days cycling, having a route which took us on a large highway and only managing one night in a tent before we chose to upgrade to a hotel.

We had spied a McDonalds just up the road from the hotel but we just couldn't bring ourselves to eat there. Yes we needed calories but we needed good nutritional food, not food that just smelt good. Fortunately there was a Lidl next to the McDonalds, our favourite small German supermarket. We purchased dinner then went back to the hotel to collapse onto the beds, stretch, wash, and watch the final of Wimbledon on the TV. Unfortunately Andy Murray lost, that's all I can remember soon after the third set I drifted into a deep, deep sleep.

Vive La France
Cycling Day 3
Saint-Jean-de-Luz to Geaune

The deep sleep was interrupted sporadically through the night. Tom's snoring never ceased and I was not able to have the comfortable night's sleep I had dreamed of. I needed to get some earplugs. I had become very dehydrated during the night and had to get up a few times to drink. However admittedly I would take it any day over those dogs from day one.

When we finally woke properly it was seven o'clock. Somehow during the few hours we had spent in the hotel we had managed to decant the entire contents of our panniers onto the bedroom floor, beds, bathroom and cupboards. Quite how, I am not sure. Needless to say, it was a slow start. After the bad nights sleep I had endured yet again, I was feeling very ill. Tom looked no better; he had huge bags under his eyes and looked totally fatigued. It seemed the shock of pushing big miles with heavily laden bike was catching up with us. The only problem was we hadn't started the really big mileage days yet. I could only imagine how bad we would be after those days. Then it hit me a wave of sickness that I wouldn't escape all morning. I rushed to the window, flipped it open, and hurled outside. My sick splattered down onto the floor below. I decided it would be a good idea for me to stay near the window and get some fresh air. I was worried; my cold if anything was getting worse. I remember thinking to myself, 'How on earth can I complete this trip in this state?' Well I would just have to. After a few more 'incidents' out of the window I was still feeling nauseas but had to pack my bike. I popped some paracetamol and set about strapping everything on, whilst dashing back to the window every couple of minutes.

It was a sad moment leaving that hotel room. We both knew it would probably be the last time we would stay in a bed until we got to Nice in the south of France. That seemed like a long way away, which it was. Reluctantly passing the sweet smell of breakfast, which we opted not to pay extra for, we hopped on our bikes. However not before, yes you guessed it; I threw up in the flowerbed. After that we thought it best to make a swift exit of the grounds.

Fortunately the hotel was right on our route, so after about 30 seconds of pedalling around the car park we were back on the road we needed to be on, the D810. France has a huge network of roads and luckily most of them can be cycled on. Basically if your road starts with a D then it will mostly be quite quiet, although this can vary a lot! If your road starts with an N then you will be very aware of this because there will most likely be large flurries of trucks and heavier traffic —these roads are only for the brave. If the road you are cycling on starts with an A then something really has gone wrong because you have found yourself on a motorway, good luck with that.

The D810 is one of the more busy D-roads as it follows the A63, which means there is a lot of motorway traffic.

However it is not a dual carriageway and early in the morning the traffic was very light. Tom had obviously woken up in an innovative mood. We both had legs that felt very heavy so he suggested that instead of grinding away on the 'big cog' all day we should shift down to the small one and ride much easier gears just spinning our legs. Today was meant to be fairly flat, so it seemed like a cop out to me. However the easy gear whilst spinning our legs was just what we needed to recover and get into the swing of things. Tom's other idea was instead of pushing long hours on the bike, only stopping to eat, we would take a break for five minutes every 40 minutes. The idea was this small break would allow us to eat more food throughout the day but also it would give us small goals to work towards which would break up the cycling. It worked. We were resting more but we were also covering more, getting a lot of quick miles done. The small breaks every 40 minutes were amazing, why hadn't we been doing this all the time? They made the cycling so much more manageable, giving us short-term goals to push off and towards. The breaks also meant our legs were more rested giving our bodies a chance to get the lactic acid out that had built up. We were more powerful, more rested, and our moods had improved a lot. The small cog was working and slowly our morale was picking up. We had a rhythm. Small chunks, breaking up the day so we could travel bigger distances.

Before we knew it we had travelled through Bayonne and were heading towards Peyrehorade and Orthez. On our third break we were running low on food so stopped at a lovely little boulangerie in a tiny village where it seemed to be the only shop alongside a post-office. We rolled up to the front door, despite the presumed smallness of the village it appeared business was booming. A group of small children quickly exited, baguettes in arms, jumped on their little bicycles and raced off home across the empty road. Tom was the first to venture inside the small homely bakery, clutching his wallet. Moments later he was out with two baguettes in his arms, one for now and one for lunch. It was now my turn, feeling adventurous I went for "Deux pain aux chocolates et une baguette". It was a good call, as I was exiting the shop the warm pastry was already making its way up towards my mouth. Oozing chocolate into my mouth, the taste sensation exploded, this was a true French breakfast now. After a few short minutes our breakfast had disappeared, barely touching the sides I might add. However rather than be greedy we decided to turn our attention to what we needed, water. Fortunately as this was the only shop in the town it did also have bottles of water, and they were cheap. Brimming our water bottles and strapping more to our panniers using our bungee cords. Then feeling substantially heavier than we did fifteen minutes ago we mounted our bikes and pushed off.

Now it felt like we were finding our rhythm we were able to converse more whilst cycling. Rather than dwell on the negatives or the pain of cycling we could focus on the trip and experiences that we were having or that we might have. We made an effort of looking for potential rough camping spots all day, just to make us more familiar with what to look for and where we might find them. It was almost getting fun now. The roads were never too busy, which is always great, it helped relieve any stress.

Although I still felt very ill, now that we had found our groove I found it much easier to ignore it. Yes, every now and again I would almost hurl however just chatting to Tom made it a whole lot easier, and those breaks worked a charm.

I did find myself sporadically counting down the minutes till the next break, wishing for it to come sooner. However the moment the next forty minutes started I found myself in a whole different mindset. I began to think about how odd it was that I could feel such contrasting extremes of emotions, over such short periods of time. How one moment I would feel so rubbish that I was considering throwing in the towel; the next I was enjoying it so much I felt I could continue on cycling around the world. It was a strange sensation, which I had never experienced before. I think the chronic tiredness was beginning to sink in; with the stress of the previous two days, along with the nagging thoughts of 'where would we sleep tonight?'

As the day progressed we began to realise how we were making such fast miles. This due to our new found rhythm and also due to it being a very flat day compared to the previous two. We only had to do 800 metres of ascent today, wahoo! It was a grey muggy day in France, although despite the lack of sunshine it was pleasantly warm. Not too hot but comfortably in the late teens early twenties, perfect for some long distance cycling. At times it appeared that the clouds were going to part, opening up a vast expanse of blue, they didn't. Fortunately this did not faze us as we sped to our lunch spot, just outside of Orthez.

We had covered nearly 93 kilometres! It wasn't even one o'clock. This was working now. This was what the cycle tour was meant to be like. Quick and fun. The roads were lovely and quiet except from the occasional truck. However I think we had seen more trucks since entering France a day earlier than my whole history of cycling in Britain.

'Where are they all coming from?' I jokingly asked Tom. 'It's like every Frenchman drives a truck instead of a car!'

Our lunch spot was at a small bus stop surrounded by fields, very green and very picturesque. I was eating my staple of Baguette and water, interspersed with a few sweets here and there. Tom joined me, having two baguettes; we were certainly eating our much needed calories. Tom was already planning dinner as we sat on the rough asphalt and ate lunch. We decided because we had made such good progress we could afford to relax for a short while and have an extended lunch. It was music to my ears; I lay back and basked in the dull midday warmth, jumping up sporadically every time a truck hurtled past.

The lunch gave us a chance to talk about how our journey was going. We both agreed that it was much harder than we thought it was going to be. We had anticipated a gentle cycle across Europe, drinking, eating, and meeting new people. At this moment we had done very little of any. We realised how we were in dire need of a good nights sleep so made it our plan to find somewhere to camp early, rather than push on and do more miles. We had about two hours left riding. This was a reassuring realisation and did give us a piece of mind. In a way it felt like the hardest part of the day was over. The hardest part of the trip however, we knew that would be the Alps. With some huge mountain passes planned, I was almost certain I would not be able to make it if my current virus-ridden state did not improve. That lunch we stumbled across a phrase which would stick with us the whole journey. We decided from now on we would just 'take it as it comes'.

Those five words were great, they let us relax, not dwell on the future but to live in the present. We were free. Released from the bounds of the 3000 kilometres we had to cycle. Now we were just cycling, the distance and where we were headed were no longer the obsession, we were cycling here.

I was feeling heaps better than I did in the morning, the bike being the cure for my virus, keeping it at bay. We really enjoyed those kilometres after lunch, pedalling down the D983, scenic and peaceful. The sun almost came out. We were tired but we had had our first great day cycling. We may have felt terrible, barely surviving off the bike. On the bike was a different matter, it healed us, gave us a place to recover, something else to focus on. When we were on the bikes we were no longer ill or stranded 3000 kilometres from a finish line. We were two 17 year old best friends, pedalling through France on their summer holidays. Sublime.

The afternoon drifted away along with the kilometres. We stopped once at an Aldi, in our first break after lunch, to replenish our water however made the call not to buy food as we still had 30 kilometres left to cycle that day.

'We'll surely find loads more shops during those 30 kilometres', we agreed.

25 kilometres later and we had been past nowhere useful for collecting supplies. We had cycled through some

lovely walled towns however no super-marché's. It wasn't even 4pm though so we felt we had nothing to worry about. Every extra kilometre we cycled today would come off tomorrows, another great motivating statement of the trip. Fortunately we got lucky when we cycled through the town of Geaune. In keeping with all the other villages and towns we had cycled through that afternoon Geaune was an old stone built town, with its fair share of cobbles. Cycling around we thought we were yet again out of luck. When just as we were pedalling out of the main square I eye-spied a Spar. Hallelujah! We could eat. Not only that, but there was a boulangerie next door. It was Tom's turn to buy provisions. He came out with a more modest amount of food this time. However it all looked great, we were already salivating at this point. Looking like a pair of hungry stray dogs, as we departed Geaune in search of a camping spot.

Determined to find a wild camping spot today we were going to settle for nothing less. However it was only just past four, this was going to make it difficult to avoid being seen. Fortunately we seemed to be on a roll. Having covered our target mileage for the day just a few kilometres earlier, we found our camping spot. We had taken the habit of stopping at every farm track. One of us would stay with the bikes while the other would scour the land looking for suitable sites. If they thought they had found one the other one would go and check. If we both agreed –I was usually the one to disagree, Tom was happy anywhere- then we would set up and camp there. Fortunately on the second stop we found a superb spot in a field. It wasn't being cultivated so we figured it would be okay to camp in; it was raised up a dirt track from the road so we definitely wouldn't be seen. Our grass coloured tent along with our camouflage tarpaulins would help with that too. Stealthily moving our gear and bikes from the road to the top end of the field, to avoid being seen by anyone, we quickly had set up camp.

Although the field looked great on first inspection, it was rutted with hundreds of root stumps where it had previously been cultivated, not ideal sleeping conditions. As was becoming the theme of the day we got lucky, finding an area free of roots and flies. Dinner time. Tom's plan of minestrone soup with the bread he bought, some chicken instant noodles, and bananas was great. A delicious Michelin star quality meal, yet with huge portions. We weren't the only ones enjoying it either. The ants could evidently smell the wondrous aromas that were escaping from the pan too and flocked to us in their hundreds. However they found it difficult to get onto the tarp so didn't bother us too much, lucky again.

Dinner devoured, pots cleaned, only one thing left to do, collapse into our sleeping bags. I had never been more comfortable until that point. It may have been only 5:30 however we still found it very easy to slip into a deep coma of relaxation.

We Just Love To Cycle
Cycling Day 4
Geaune to Grenade

Despite falling to sleep quickly I woke many times during the night. This was due to the great orchestra which emanated from Tom's nose when he fell asleep. I desperately needed some earplugs for sleeping. However I still managed to have the best night's sleep of the trip so far, although I was still feeling ill I felt I was improving. The bike surely was healing me, so were the copious amounts of ibuprofen and paracetamol I was ingesting.

We woke early. Keen to get in a big day of cycling, today we were aiming for 160 kilometres. At 6:45 the alarm went off on Tom's phone and we opened our eyes to the misty world outside. A quick breakfast of left over bread was all that was on offer. However being greedy teenagers we leapt at it and it was gone in a matter of minutes. We dressed quickly; it was simple as we just wore what we had on the day before. There was no way we could carry a months worth of cycling clothes. I don't even think I own a weeks worth, so we had no choice but to be smelly. We did have a couple of changes, though these were being saved for key events. One pair of clothes per week, surely that would be fine? Although today was day four and there was a definite odd smell present. Fingers crossed for the next three weeks.

We had definitely got packing up camp perfected to a fine art now, although this was only our second night in the wild. We managed to have bikes loaded and by the roadside at 7:30, an early start for us.

We left no trace of our camping ground, taking all litter with us to put in the next available bin. That is one of the most important things I have found about wild camping, respecting the area in which you camp. It is not your right to camp there, although I do think it everyone's right as a human to have somewhere to sleep. If you are considerate of the land, people will be considerate of you. What goes around comes around in essence. I think leaving no trace is a key part of that, it means if more travellers wish to stay in the same place after you they will not be shooed away because you had not respected the land.

Hopping on the bikes we started our first 40 minutes, along the D2 towards Aire-sur-l'Adour. It was lovely cycling, mainly flat with the odd challenging climb thrown in. All the time the road was weaving through huge forests and fields, more shades of green than my eyes could perceive. The roads were near empty as it was early in the morning for France.

We started to cycle past lots of signs for 'Fois Gras'. For those of you who don't know what that is, it translates as 'fat liver' into English. It is the liver of a duck or goose that has been specially fattened by force feeding, many of the birds have their feet nailed to wooden boards and tubes for feeding inserted down their throats. I am not going to get into the whole controversy of the food but it is a well know delicacy in French cuisine. However for me knowing how it was prepared I couldn't stomach buying some to taste it, I also was brought up a vegetarian so have a weak stomach for meat anyway.

After our second 40 minutes we reached Aire-sur-l'Adour and it was time to buy some proper breakfast. Also Tom was running low on water so we were lucky, yet again, when we spotted signs for an Aldi. I don't know what we would've done on this cycling trip without small German supermarket chains. They always turned up when times were hard. From 0.16€ two litre bottles of water to fresh pain au chocolates, they always had something we craved. They enabled us to spend less than 5€ on food per day yet still eat 3 huge meals. They were our backbone and for this I thank them.

After the brief break, guess what? We started cycling again. Is it getting a little repetitive now? It almost was for us as well. Let's see how we were after another three weeks of it. The stop had been good; we had found some Haribo which was a great snack whilst on the bike, it gave us a nice quick sugar fix. The roads were great and we quickly found ourselves amused by dramatically saying song lyrics instead of singing songs whilst cycling. It may sound very odd but before you judge us try it for yourself. Imagine you are reading the lyrics as a poem or a speech, it sounds odd. However on reflection we may have just started to go a little crazy at this point. Who knows? We had had very little contact -bar ourselves- with the outside world in almost a week. I think it was beginning to show.

At our next break I decided to look ahead at the route. Suddenly a sinking feeling overwhelmed me. Please not a repeat of two days earlier on the Spanish motorway. Fingers crossed it wouldn't, however it looked like we were about to join a very busy N-road. This is the part in the movies where the character swallows and the audience hears a large gulping sound. Fingers crossed. Tentatively we cycled on, feeling reassured that we hadn't died in Spain so we wouldn't in France, good logic I know. I knew we were technically allowed to cycle on N-roads in France however this looked like a particularly big one as it had junctions and was quite wide on the map. As we joined the road our worst fears were realised. It was busy. Trucks and cars hurtling down it. We had no option but to gun it. The 60-90 kilometre stint had always been the hardest section of the day and today was definitely no exception. The foray of French car horns had begun, the crescendo of the symphony deafened us. Some seemed to be congratulatory, some seemed to be angry, and they all were annoying. Being from England we have the most opposite horn culture, a rarity to hear a horn beep; we found it hard to get adjusted to this new custom. We pedalled hard, taking little account of where we were cycling through, keen to get off the road. Fortunately bigger roads tend to be flatter, so we were able to keep a fast speed. However the long ascents were tiring on our legs and meant our speed was much lower than the other road vehicles. As there were either two or three lanes all the time this did mean that cars had plenty of space to pass, so there were only a few close encounters.

It was now nearing lunch; we were finally approaching the 90 kilometre mark. However we were still cycling on the N-124, we had just passed Auch (our legs thought this town was aptly named) and saw signs that Le Tour de France was passing through our very route in just a couple of days time. Taking a quick picture of the sign we sprinted on, with a new found love of where we were. It felt special to be riding the same roads just a few days before stage 15 would start. After that stage Bradley Wiggins would be winning and in the yellow jersey with a 2'05" advantage over fellow teammate Chris Froome. It was an exciting experience being in France during Le Tour, especially as Wiggo would eventually go on to win and be the first Brit to do so. It was a good time to be English, cycling, and in France.

With 15 kilometres to go on the N-124 we were tired and losing morale. The constant orchestra of horns and stress of the busy road were taking their toll. We neared a lay-by and decided to stop for lunch. It was not fun. Just like that a good morning had gone bad. We were once again feeling pessimistic about the trip and about the day. The grey skies echoed our feelings. We ate lunch quickly all the while being barraged by turbulence from passing trucks. We both lay back on the rough asphalt, knackered. However this was hardly the best place to 'relax'. I looked how much further we had on this godforsaken road, 15 kilometres. That would take us over the magic 100 kilometre mark. After a very quick lunch we got straight back on the bikes and pushed hard. We were not going to stop till we made it to the refuge of quieter roads.

Those last 15 kilometres were a blur, I am pretty sure I was seeing black spots across my vision. We encountered some road works for one section which was a relief as there was a lower speed limit. Finally after about 45 minutes we escaped. Phew. Our day could only get better from here.

The quieter roads were heaven; never again will they be taken for granted. We spotted a lovely lay-by encased by sunflower fields and decided to take a much needed celebratory break, and photos. We had now covered over 100 kilometres, all plain sailing from here. The day was still early too. This was turning into the fastest day so far. We basked in our glory whilst calmly pedalling through the sunflower fields. Things were definitely beginning to take a turn for the better. Our daily mileages were increasing, our routine was more regular and the cycling, camping and adjustment was getting easier. Today we would hit 160 kilometres again and it felt good. This was the goal, if we could achieve it this early, by the end it would be a piece of cake –in theory.

Alarmingly we soon realised we hadn't seen a shop since the Aldi in the morning; we were running dangerously low on water. Fortunately we came across a petrol station, in the middle of nowhere, which sold small bottles of water. They were ridiculously overpriced and unfortunately the woman wouldn't fill up our bottles from her tap, despite our best efforts of persuasion. We settled for the expensive water, needs must.

We ate up those final few miles and before we knew it we had covered 160 kilometres, two days in a row! It was now time to start looking for some food and a place to camp. Away from major cities the latter should be easy we thought. Luckily it was. Within a few minutes of pedalling through French farmland we had found what looked like a perfect spot. It was an empty field, accessible by jumping over a small stream. Made invisible by surrounding trees, what could be better? It was only four in the afternoon but we could relax. It felt amazing. Unloading the bikes, Tom took the big leap over the stream, a precarious jump as it was in a 6 foot ditch that was over a metre across. Luckily he made it easily and I began throwing gear over to him. We decided to lock the bikes to a tree rather than haul them over too. Covering them in a camouflage tarpaulin, they should be out of sight we thought. Putting up the tent we suddenly realised what a bad decision we had made. Flies. They were everywhere, crawling, buzzing; now we could not relax. We persevered putting the tent up to take refuge. However we knew we could not stay there. It would be impossible to cook or eat. Therefore one of us had to make the call. Should we stay or should we go? Reluctantly after a lot of deliberating we made the call that had to be made, we departed.

Fleeing the campsite was hard. It was demoralising packing down and setting off not knowing where we would be sleeping and if anything else was ahead. I immediately questioned and regretted the decision. What if we couldn't find anywhere? What if...? The questions built up and overwhelmed my thinking. Our cycling was slow and lethargic. We had already cycled 160 kilometres and our bodies didn't want to do anymore. That was enough. We had cycled a further five kilometres and still nothing. This was alarming, we had been spying camping spots all day and now we couldn't see anything. Everywhere was flat, barren and relatively lifeless. This meant no cover to camp, something we still felt we needed to wild camp. A once great end to the day was spiralling downhill, depression was hitting. We looked ahead at the map and saw we were about to hit the city of Grenade. Yes we could get some much needed food but where would we be able to camp in a city? Slim pickings we thought.

The sun was getting lower and the day darker, along with our thoughts. I was feeling low now. We had cycled 170 kilometres and still nowhere to stay. Why did we have to leave that campsite? Damning questions that made my thoughts drop lower and I then began to think of home. I had never been homesick before in my life. I had been away for many weeks at a time from my family and home but never did I miss the comfort and security of it like I did then. A huge sinking feeling welled inside me, what had I let myself into here? I began thinking that this could be the end of the trip; I could not go on in this state. I slowly began to realise that the really tough thing about long expeditions is being mentally strong and prepared. We had done no preparation physically let alone mentally. The cycling was fine now; it was the mental struggles of every day that were the testing and tough parts. It definitely requires a certain type of person to not always dwell on the negatives and to be positive even though they fear the worst. I think Tom sensed my disheartenment so when we finally reached civilisation and a supermarché he did what I needed. Consoling, motivation and smiles, everything was not all lost.

However there was some part of me inside that was still broken and lost. So I was reconciled when I switched my phone on and read encouraging texts from family and friends. However this did have the effect of making me miss home life even more. Never have I appreciated a warm bed, roof over my head, home cooked meals or even running water. I longed for the structure and regiment of a normal life, what I was experiencing in Europe I had never experienced before. I did not know what was coming round the next bend; there was no ability of foresight. You had to live in the here and now; I was definitely finding this a tough transition. As a person I like to be organised and always know what is going to happen so I think this made it even harder. In order to cope I would have to change my whole personality. If I succeeded then that would definitely be for the better. It was day four, I only had two options; change and carry on or fail, bail on the adventure and get a plane home. However I also am not a quitter, if I have a challenge to complete I will complete it. This mentality was stronger, so I realised I only had one option, to continue. The realisation of how tough this was going to be mentally hit me hard.

Immediately after realising this, my phone began vibrating in my hands. My mum was ringing. This was the first time I had spoken to her since waving good-bye to board the ferry. I was not prepared. I couldn't worry her because then she would get really worried but then I couldn't lie to her. When I answered the phone she knew something was up. So I told her everything. How I was homesick, how I still had the flu, how it was really tough, how I no longer had a back break, how we had nowhere to sleep. I can imagine it was quite a load to listen to, especially as she was relatively helpless to give us any aid.

However speaking out my problems was a weight lifted from my shoulders. The homesickness wasn't helped at first; I just missed home even more. However by the end of that conversation I felt a changed boy. I would 'take it as it comes' and make it around Europe.

I went in to the supermarket and purchased some much needed dinner, chicken cous cous and a chicken salad baguette both were delicious. It was still light so I sent the dark thoughts about finding a place to sleep to the back of my mind and focused on the positives. I was in France on my summer holiday doing the thing that I loved with my best friend. From here on in it was just going to get better and better. Just like that my mood totally swapped, Tom had a similar experience and we were both feeling on top of the world again. It's an odd thing what stress can do to the body, all you need to do is just think logically, live in the present and not dwell on the negatives. Fortunately I was now beginning to learn this valuable lesson.

As dusk approached we decided we had better cycle on and look for a place to camp. We stopped often however Grenade is a large town and so there were no good spaces. One place looked promising as it looked out of the way, however on close inspection it looked like a popular spot for local dog walkers and youths. We deciphered this because of the amount of dog droppings and beer cans. That made me think we were yet to have a proper drink on this trip, hardly the classic teenagers the newspapers describe. Just before we crossed La Garrone, the river that runs through Grenade, we pulled over because I needed a wee. I hopped down the slope of the road and did my business, it was then I realised I couldn't see the road or Tom. I had found it. The perfect camping spot. In a sunflower field there was a space to put the tent which because of and area of trees next to the field was enclosed on all sides. We had sunflowers on three of our sides and trees on one side; you wouldn't have known we were barely out of Grenade.

This was by far the best camping site of the trip so far. All the sunflowers were in full bloom making it a sunny haven of tranquillity. We were about 200 metres from the river and the rowing club. As Tom and I are rowers we found this last fact very interesting, we are very cool teenagers we know. Before we knew it we had transported all our luggage and bikes to the spot and had our tent up. The sun was now setting, sending the sky blood-red and crimson. We brushed our teeth and settled in to our new home. Once inside the tent we were completely invisible, the tent was the same colour as the grass and the bikes were hidden underneath a camouflage tarp with the trees. Just got to hope the farmer doesn't decide to do a late night harvest I thought to myself.

We talked for a bit, read our books and send texts to our families and girlfriends. Before we knew it, once again we drifted into stupors having cycled 176 kilometres. That was a big day.

The Sun has Arrived
Cycling Day 5
Grenade to Saint-Martin-de-l'Arçon

We were finally settling into the daily routine of life on the road. Alarm goes off just before 7, wake up, get dressed and pack up the inside of the tent. Make it outside for some quick relief, then brush teeth and have breakfast. After this, we would begin taking down the tent, packing up panniers and other luggage, then begin transporting everything from the camping spot back to the road, making sure no rubbish is left behind. It was a simple process however we only rarely managed it in under an hour. I am a morning person. I don't always like that I am a morning person and I know those around me in the morning do not appreciate it. However it does have its divine uses. Once I am awake I am wide awake. Bang, the alarm goes off, I am already upright and getting dressed. Although I may still feel tired there's nothing I can do once I awaken. Fortunately for Tom I was one of these people. Tom is almost the opposite, he loves his bed. To be honest who can blame him when you've cycled 160 odd kilometres the previous day! This was where we worked well as a team, and I could put my early starts to good use rallying Tom making sure we got on our bikes quickly and got in some good early miles before the midday heat.

Day five was very much the same as usual. I woke quickly to the sound of Tom's alarm and nudged him. I had been nudging him all night as his snoring had gotten out of control! I was woken several times to the thunderous roar coming out of his nostrils. It was after about the third time I decided to turn my MP3 player on and fall to sleep listening to that rather than Tom's sporadic snoring. This seemed to have worked although it wasn't the comfiest; my ears were hurting. I made a mental note to myself to try harder to look for earplugs at supermarkets, kicking myself for not buying some before we left England.

By 8 o'clock we were pedalling over La Garrone and out of Grenade. It was now time to start track two of the route on the GPS. A momentous occasion to start the day to. It finally felt we were making a small dint on our trip around Europe. Next goal the Mediterranean. Leaving Grenade the traffic was very heavy. It was rush hour and there were plenty of cars making their way to Toulouse which was only about 30 kilometres away. We had decided not to go via Toulouse as it would be a 50 kilometre detour and a slow, busy one at that. We were really enjoying the relaxing winding D-roads, which wound their way across France through the small towns experiencing true French culture, that was what we were doing it for. I think we were also mainly doing it for the challenge, two 17 year olds jumping on their bikes with a few Euros, who really thought we were going to make it? I knew my parents definitely had doubts. That was another reason, I don't like people telling me I can't do something, call me stubborn but I just don't like it. I have to prove them wrong. There it was; I was cycling around Europe to prove that it is easy, anyone can do it no matter what, it doesn't require much planning or money and you will have a great time at the end of it. Well so far I wasn't really proving anyone wrong, it was hard. However we were yet to give up, we had already been through some very hard times and we were still going. We weren't finished with Europe yet. These thoughts filled my head throughout the morning and I basked in satisfaction and new found confidence. We could actually do this. Yes our planning hadn't been great and that had shown on the first few days. However we were now nearing a week of constant cycling. We were beginning to adapt, to change as people; we were now stronger mentally and physically. Today we were going to have fun.

In the morning we flew, cycling through the heart of French countryside, every other field was filled with sunflowers. To add to the brightness the sun was now truly shining, you could tell we were getting further south. It was heating up. Time to get the tan on. Tom joked that the only reason he came on this trip was to get some unbelievable tan lines. Well if the weather stayed like this for the next 18 days then we just might.

The morning was wondrous, lovely weather and roads. Although we were on a busier N-road for quite a bit we were heading away from Toulouse so there was little traffic in our direction to bother us. It seemed the tides were turning, although I have said that many times we were actually beginning to believe it this time. We saw many lovely people who wished us well on our journey, our GCSE French was beginning to come back to us now and our once pigeon French was becoming slightly more fluent, so that we could string together a brief conversation.

However although we thought GCSE French had prepared us, unbeknown to us we had no conversations describing the different rooms in our houses or what we like to do on the weekend, nor were we asked to compare Manchester to a French town. All our vocabulary learning had been for nothing.

We managed to score some food for lunch in a lovely supermarket in Mazamet. The first French supermarket on our trip to stock Baked Beans, what a result! We cycled on a few more kilometres then stopped on a farm track to bask in the hot midday sun and eat our treasures. The baked beans were particularly tasty. We had already cycled over 100 kilometres; it had been a very fast morning. Our superb camping spot the previous night had obviously done its trick; I also think the weather had something to do with it. Just under 60 kilometres to go and the whole of the afternoon to do it in, now we could relax. Tom lay down to work on his tan while I looked ahead at the route. We had been cycling down a huge valley all day in the 'Parc naturel régional du Haut-Languedoc' we were cycling at the foot of the Montagne Noire mountain range. It seemed it would never end; surely sometime we would have to cycle up over it to get out of this valley. However I was reassured when I saw the road we were going to join passed along a river so couldn't be that hilly.

After the heat of the day had passed we decided we had better get back to cycling, although it was lovely to have a long relaxed lunch. Those next few kilometres were some of the most pretty of the trip so far. Mountains all around, fields and rivers flowing in the valley along with rich wildlife fluttering all around. It was truly paradise.

The amount of RV's and motor homes that were on the roads clearly indicated that the French knew this as well. I was falling in love with the cycling today. This was how I envisaged the whole trip being, sun shining and relaxed pedalling.

Yet although we were in paradise in a national park this had not deterred McDonalds from infiltrating, rather than ignore this eyesore in the lovely countryside we decided to make good use of flushing toilets while we could. After a short interlude we were on the bikes again feeling much more relieved.

We had been talking a lot about Top Gear today along with the usual Lord of the Rings chatter. Those were the only two topics we ever seemed to talk about in great detail. I find this very odd looking back as although they are both very enjoyable I still cannot fathom how we managed to have such in-depth conversations about them for probably what added up to over 100 hours over the whole month. I think by this stage we had perhaps gone a little crazy.

We covered the next 50 kilometres in about two hours, despite them all being uphill. As we only had 10 kilometres left and we had gone so far yesterday we did not want to push on and injure ourselves so we had a slightly lighter day of cycling, although that still involved cycling 160 kilometres. Rather than cycle on we took another break. We stopped in the town of Saint-Pons-de-Thomières, a quaint old town. We sat on a bench and listened to Tom's iPod for almost an hour while we 'people watched' and had some brief conversations with locals. This was what I had imagined the trip would be like, cycling and chilling, the only way it could've been better was if I had had a lovely cold beer to cool me down. Fortunately we were sat in the shade because this certainly had turned out to be one hot day.

When we started again we began looking for camping spots, it took us the usual 10 kilometres to find somewhere suitable but not ideal. We found a car park for a white water rafting club. When we arrived we presumed everyone would be leaving soon as it wasn't that busy. No one presented themselves that we could ask about camping. We decided to not put up camp and to just cook a meal then see if people had disappeared by then. The curry was good, one of the best meals so far. It seemed we were finally getting the hang of cooking on a tiny stove, if I do say so myself. We had plenty of rice too which filled us well. My cold had improved a lot today; I was a lot less bunged up and only had the occasional cough. At six o'clock our worst fears were realised. They weren't going to leave; this was too open to set up camp. We had one option to carry on and look for another place to camp. This resonated with the feelings of yesterday; it was yet again a hard decision to make. Especially as the sun was setting and because we were still in the valley the sun would set quickly.

We were efficient. Bags all packed and onto the bikes in under ten minutes. Then we pedalled. Legs feeling fresh from the meal we had in our stomachs we pushed hard, stopping readily to check out spots behind bushes and down tracks. Nearing an hour later we had found nothing. It was getting worryingly dark now. It would soon be night, then finding a good place and setting up would be even harder. We persevered though, not going to give up easily. We took to cycling up nearby roads seeing if tracks led off them, all with no luck. Everywhere was cliffs or steep hillside, hardly ideal for pitching a tent. Luckily just as the last slither of sun disappeared from view we found what we had been looking for.

It was off a quieter road and was almost completely out of sight. Although there were signs of previous human disturbance —broken beer bottles and squashed cans- we decided it was here or nowhere. So we set up camp. There was a lot of wildlife in this area and we were careful to make sure the tent was securely locked up as lots of ants and spiders had come out to play. Once erected, the tent as usual blended in completely. We had done it. Our first fantastic day, yes we had had some hard times but they were minute compared with previous days, also we had dealt with our daily challenges well. As I lay back on my Thermarest I took out the GPS to look at tomorrow's route. We were about 50 kilometres from the Mediterranean. Tomorrow we would reach our first major destination of this trip. I couldn't wait. With positive thoughts filling my head, I fell asleep, as usual, to the sound of Tom's snoring.

The Plague of the Mosquitoes
Cycling Day 6
Saint-Martin-de-l'Arçon to Saintes-Maries-De-La-Mer

I woke with positive thoughts still filling my head, although to add to the sound of Tom's snoring, the alarm was bleeping away. Tom had been suffering on the hard ground because his Thermarest had decided it didn't enjoy having air in it. There must have been a minute puncture in it because it only stayed inflated for a couple of hours. However a couple of hours are hardly ideal when you're aiming for a good nights sleep. We arose to quite a chilly morning however there were no clouds so we were sure once the sun was in the air it would get pretty hot. Once we had clambered out of our tent we could properly inspect our camping spot. Hardly the best place we had camped, there were brambles and nettles everywhere; I cut myself a few times. However there were less 'creepy crawlies' this morning, which was good. That is one thing which Tom and I were not looking forward to about the camping, bugs. More specifically mosquitoes, these little flies we were worried about, I particularly seem to have some special bond with them as I always get bitten. However we had avoided them so far and we weren't expecting to have any problems, if any, till we hit Italy.

We were quick to get going and on the bikes within 45 minutes. We had about 80 kilometres to the Med and we were both really keen to make it there by lunch. This filled us with anticipation of not having any climbing; we were presuming it would be mostly flat cycling. From entering France up until this point we hadn't had any climbs that rivalled the first couple of days, it had just been undulating or flat, which meant the miles were covered fast. Although yesterday had felt like a flat day we actually had hit our highest altitude on the GPS of 500 metres. Probably a mere bump compared to what was to come in the Alps I thought. As we had risen early –like always- the roads were empty. We were riding through the same region as yesterday and it was quiet and lovely. Classic small French villages nestled in the hillsides, rustic would describe them perfectly. We had looked ahead and saw the road we were following left the river and began to turn quite a bit, so we were expecting hills. We couldn't stay in this valley forever.

As we had no breakfast and hadn't spotted anywhere we were running on empty at this point. Our aim today was to camp somewhere on the Med then tomorrow after a week of cycling finally take our first proper 'rest' day and cycle what was left to Saintes-Marie-De-La-Mer; relax on the beach there. We had seen wonderful pictures of this place and the roads looked divine, I personally was looking forward to it. It was a slight detour to go down to visit it however I hoped it would be worth it. I think Tom was also looking forward to a rest day. The cycling was having a profound effect on our bodies; it was slowly wearing them away, body and mind. I felt a rest day was duly needed; we had been going to near hell this past week and had plundered on relentlessly. We needed time to relax, take in where we were and enjoy the Med. With that goal in mind we were cycling hard, 40 minutes on 5 minutes off. It was amazing how well this system worked. Definitely the rhythm for us, it kept us 'sane'.

I lost Tom once early on during the morning; a bottle fell from his rear pannier so he stopped to pick it up. As I was in front I did not realise this until five minutes later when I found I had been just talking to myself -silly me. I stopped, looked round and couldn't see him; I was on a long straight road which made it increasingly worrying. I decided to retrace my steps, or pedal strokes whichever you prefer, to go find him. I was worrying now, what if he had carried on the wrong direction looking for me. We had just passed through the small town of Hérépian and turned off the D908 to join the D909A, what if it had happened before this. I cycled all the way back to the junction. There, thank god, was Tom. He had decided just to wait, knowing that I would realise eventually. We joked about how bad that could've turned out and then carried on up. Yes up. The road had begun to rise now. It looked like we were going to have to go over the mountains rather than under or through them. Wahoo! Not.

They kept on rising, as did the temperature. It was turning into yet another lovely day, hopefully one of many to come. As we were cycling up the final climb of the morning we were both looking forward to the moment when we would reach the top and be able to see the Med. Unfortunately our eyesight could not stretch 30 kilometres although we were rewarded with a fantastic view and a huge decent. Instead of curving its way down the hillside the road split into two lanes and plummeted straight down. This was what we had been looking forward to, descents like these. We quickly changed up, span our legs and then let our bikes free-wheel as our pedalling was futile. We managed to hit just over 70 kph on that downhill, thank god we didn't fall off. Then disaster! No, we didn't fall off. Instead we had realised that we were meant to turn off the descent half way down. So reluctantly we turned the bikes around and started pedalling back up the steep precipice. It wasn't too bad though because our bodies were still pumping with adrenaline from the descent. Also when we made the turning we noticed a tiny little boulangerie. Finally time to go get some breakfast. Need I say the pain au chocolates were divine. Definitely the best ones so far. Freshly baked and still warm, the melted chocolate was oozing out of their core.

After breakfast we continued to cycle the final few kilometres to the coast. It was constantly undulating which actually made for very tiring cycling. Added to this we were battling against a head wind coming from the coast. To our shock we cycled past a pharmacy, who knew they had pharmacies in France? No, the shocking part was they were displaying the current temperature; it was 28 degrees! It was barely even 10; boy this was going to be some sweaty cycling, as if we didn't smell bad enough already. As we were so keen to make the coast we had forgotten about our 40 minute breaks. This wasn't good. It meant our rhythm was offset and we were losing focus. In the heat this descended quickly into discomfort. The cycling was becoming arduous. We had never cycled in conditions this hot, the thermometer continued to rise, it was near unbearable. To make matters worse, we were running low on water.

After what had felt like an age of cycling, we finally made it over the last hill. Sprawled out in front of us was the crystal clear water of The Mediterranean. We had made it. With the hot summer sun beating down on us we pedalled on until we found some shade, to bask in our triumph. It felt amazing, we had dreamt about this moment for months. Now it had come true and it was almost as I had imagined it. Unfortunately we could not run down and swim in the sea, we couldn't find a beach. It was enough to be pedalling next to it though, we were happy. It was now getting unbelievably hot, easily in the mid thirties by now. Our next task was to find some water, lunch, and some more shade.

Setting off again felt good, we had accomplished our main goal for the day and one of our main goals for the trip. It actually finally felt we were making a dint on this mammoth 3000 kilometre trip around Europe. Despite all the good feelings, the south of France especially near the Med, on the way to Montpellier from Mèze along the D613, was very busy. As I have said before D-roads are normally good cycling roads however this one was far from the norm. A high volume of cars all heading to the beaches along the coast made for quite dangerous cycling. Fortunately after a few kilometres we noticed a cycle path that followed the road. Joining that was a good decision we still made good speed but we were much safer.

Just before we hit Montpellier we eye-spied an Intermarché, time for lunch. As we parked up our bikes we couldn't help but notice that there were a lot of other bikes there too. Three of which looked like they were kitted out for touring. Were we finally going to meet some other cycle-tourers? I was surprised we hadn't seen more so far. We had passed a lot of cyclists but only a couple of tourers and not had the opportunity to speak to any, apart from a crazy German man in our Bilbao hostel. Then again I think most cycle-tourers are a little bit crazy. Who else would choose to bust their ass all day long everyday and call it a 'holiday'?

Tom went in to buy some food while I waited with the bikes. Then the craziest looking man emerged from the supermarket. His hair was dirty brown, hanging long on his head, merging into his long beard. His face looked weathered by many years on the road and his eyes darted about feverishly. However he was undoubtedly a hardcore cycle-tourer. He appeared to be French when I said 'Bonjour' to him, however he was very nervous and spoke a mixture of languages, all to no avail. His bike was one of the most fully laden I had ever seen, four huge panniers all packed to the brim with extra stuff strapped on with an array of bungees. It all looked as ancient as he was. However I did envy him. I would love to pack up my life and just go off cycling indefinitely. He had clearly been on the road for many years and wasn't really in the mood for talking. After he had eaten his lunch he jumped back on his massive bike and heaved it from rest into the distance.

Then almost instantaneously the Welsh contingent arrived. I feel terrible as neither Tom nor I can remember their names. One big, one small, they rounded the corner in huffs and puffs; obviously it had been a tiring morning. The big one almost fell off his bike then lay down on the stone wall, shouting to his friend that it was his turn to get the beers. That was where we were going wrong. After introducing ourselves we got talking to the big guy about where they had come from and what they were doing. They had flown in a couple of days ago and were cycling around the Montpellier area, staying in cheap hotels rather than camping. The big one had called the little one a 'pussy' at this as he had been on many cycle tours before and camped. However this was his friend's first one and in his own words he "Had all the gear and absolutely no idea". Tom remarked on the big guys amazing tan, he was like a bronzed Greek god, hardly what you'd expect of a Welshman. However it turned out he had just got back from sailing, the lovely holiday life of a Welsh policeman. We talked for almost an hour about different cycle tours, cycling and their lives. They couldn't believe us when we told them our route calling us 'hardcore'; I think they were a little envious. They too had seen the other crazy cycle tourer and thought he was French; however he had apparently been cycling in the opposite direction yesterday to which he was cycling today. We spoke about Saintes-Maries-De-La-Mer and said how we were hoping to get near today. The big guy had been there cycling before and told us it was as lovely as we hoped. This filled us with lots of confidence. He even got out his map and showed us how close we were to it. Why try and get there in two days when if we push hard this afternoon we could have tomorrow totally off to relax by the sea. This settled it all in our minds. We were going to make it. We also decided we would take a leaf out of their books, they were having a break every hour and a beer ever two hours, the latter sounded very appetising.

After almost an hour they were off to cycle the last 20 or so kilometres of their day. We would have about 50 more to do if we wanted to make it to Saintes-Maries-De-La-Mer. We were determined to make this. It had been our most enjoyable lunch of the 'holiday' so far. It had given us a new outlook on the cycling. We realised we had lost our jokiness and our banter. We needed to rekindle that. We were now cycling along the south of France; we had found our rhythm, spoken to some fellow Brits, got our spark back. We were having the time of our lives. I had also finally managed to purchase a pair of earplugs so could not wait to have my fist non-interrupted sleep of the trip. It was going to be amazing.

We skirted round Montpellier to get to Saintes-Maries. It was lovely riding with the sea breeze, which was now no longer a head wind. Suddenly Tom swerved right into the middle of the road. I couldn't see as I was in front of him but I heard the horn of a nearby car. It turned out he had swerved to avoid a huge snake that he almost ran over. It was just basking in the hot summer sun at the side of the road. I also must've made it angry as I did not see it so must have passed very close. After what could've been a fatal mistake Tom was in need for the toilet. He literally almost pooed himself from the fright. We pulled in to a bar we were passing to use its' amenities. Luckily it was near a Lidl so we struck lucky and stocked up on lots of food. We were expecting the Camargue to be relatively free of supermarkets.

After Tom had recovered from his 'milk overload' we sluggishly got back on the bikes and by four o'clock we were entering the Camargue. The Camargue is a regional park and nature reserve located east of Montpellier on the coast of the Mediterranean. As we entered it was like stepping back in time. Beautiful pink flamingoes were dotted across the rice paddies and salt pans. Cowboys' road their dazzling white horses which we later learned were called 'Camarguais' a breed of Horse found in that region. It was beautiful and totally flat. Not a single undulation, this was easy riding. We stopped once to take some photographs of the amazing scenery and unfortunately a mosquito, the first of the trip, bit me. Keen to get away from the mosquito threat we rode on toward Saintes-Maries-De-La-Mer the capital of the Camargue region.

It did not take long, as we arrived early we decided to go for a cycle around the town rather than check into a campsite. We also decided if we could find a cheap hotel we would stay in it as we were taking the day off tomorrow. Unfortunately everywhere was full; it was peak holiday season after all. The town itself was very busy, lots of holiday makers and it felt very commercialised. A stark contrast to the area where it was situated. So we rode just out of the town and headed for a campsite we had already seen, 'Le Clos du Rhône'.

There was nowhere to rough camp in this nature reserve so we decided that it would be best to just pay for a campsite for once. However this was one of the most expensive campsites ever. We had to turn over 25€, just to put up our tiny little tent! An outrage, it better be good we thought. At least it was on the beach, had a pool and showers. It seemed a good quality campsite. I went to book us in while Tom stayed with the bikes and attempted to swat a few mosquitoes that seemed to have found us. We thought nothing of it at the time. A lovely lady showed us where to set up our tent and we were eager to put it up so we could relax. We got to our spot. Suddenly a great cloud rose up. It encircled us. Then it sent us jumping and swatting in every direction. A mosquito plague had enveloped us. We were running around, to and fro, trying to get them off our bodies. Finally after great difficulty we somehow managed to get the tent up. All the while twitching, swatting and running off. It had been a lengthy and painful process. Leaving our bikes and bags outside we took refuge inside the tent. There we could rest.

"What on earth was that?" I said to Tom, "I don't know why they are going for us and no one else". By this time everyone around us was giving us weird looks. No mosquitoes seemed to be bothering them. Why us? We decided it must be because we were so dirty so we decided to grab our towels and go for showers.

"3...2...1...Go!" Unzipping the tent and running to the shower block. We managed to not take any mosquitoes with us. Unfortunately for us the tiny bastards had infiltrated the shower block as well and were lining the ceiling. This was going to be a painful shower. Washing and swatting, that was the only way. We had to do both simultaneously to avoid being bitten. Our efforts were futile though. There were just too many and they were relentless. Even after we had dried our now clean bodies they were coming after us. I decided I would go and ask for a new camping spot that might prove luckier. It didn't. They followed us and they were already waiting for us. They were everywhere. The amount of bites on us was now not a laughing matter, we had put on our jackets yet they still penetrated through.

We decided we would have to be efficient. We grabbed the bikes locked them up, grabbed some food and our sleeping stuff and shoved it in the tent. Put a tarp over our bags then jumped into the tent. It was only six in the evening, not even remotely dark. We were in too much pain to move out of our tent. By this time the whole camping site was giving us odd looks. Luckily our tent remained a mosquito free zone. Well at least it did on the inside.

Our bodies were completely red, I found it impossible to itch because I had so many my whole body had gone numb and was tingling. Tom began counting up his bites; he had over 110 bites on his right leg alone. After this number he got bored and lost count. I had slightly less however I had reacted worse; each one of my bites had swollen up and become raised, it looked like I had hundreds of boils all over my body. It was so painful. Our bodies could not cope. It was only after we sent pictures to our families that they believed how bad it was. It is hard to comprehend or put into words just how horrendous this attack had been on us. What we couldn't understand is why they were going for us. We began to laugh about it, what else could we do but laugh? It wasn't really a laughing matter as we were in so much pain. We were really dreading tomorrow.

It had been such a good day until this point. The mistake of Le Clos du Rhône is one I will never forget. I will never be going back there, its beauty is shadowed forever in my my memories by the mosquito plague. It makes me itchy just remembering it. The writhing pain; the blood running all down my arms from where I had swatted the nasty things as they were sucking it out of me. It was a horrible experience. Not wanting to venture out of the tent into hell. We decided we would just spend the whole night in the tent. So much for going and getting some beers. We would just have to read our books and itch. Oh no sorry, 'not itch', it was just so hard. All the histamine flowing through my body as a result of the bites combined with my new earplugs meant that despite the pain I did manage to fall asleep with surprising ease.

Flight
Cycling Day 7
Saintes-Maries-De-La-Mer to Salon-de-Provence

The itching woke us. It had plagued us all night and was hurting us now. The high pitched hum outside reminded us what lay in wait. So much for a nice relaxing day off. We decided we would have to escape this place. There was no way we could spend our day off here. It would be the end of us. We carefully put on our layers of clothes and got ready to get out of the tent. Just at that point we looked up. Hundreds, if not thousands, of mosquitoes were lying in wait on the top of our tents inner layer. Biding their time to get us. 'Oh lord', we thought, this is beyond a joke now.

Our plan was simple. Get out of the tent and run to the shower block carrying whatever kit we could carry with us. There seemed to be slightly less mosquitoes there to get us. Then we would run back and forth, and begin to load the bikes whilst running around and swatting. Yes, we got a lot of funny looks.

"Look at those funny English boys running around like headless chickens", they were probably all saying to each other.

Then slowly we would take apart the tent, one layer at a time. All this took about 45 minutes. It was a pain. We were so close to freedom from this hellhole we could taste it, but we couldn't enjoy it yet. As I went to check out, the lady said we weren't allowed to check out until 8:30. What. A. Bitch. I am sorry about the swearing, I normally hate it. However we were desperate. We were in so much pain; it was unrelenting and getting worse. This woman was depriving us from our freedom, we were trapped. I told Tom the bad news whilst running laps of the shower block, waving my arms around like a mad man. Those were some long fifteen minutes. Eventually they passed though. Then we were free. Neither of us were dressed for cycling, we were wearing thicker shorts and many layers. This was not bothering us now though. We had to get out of this area and fast. We sprinted to get out of the Camargue region. Then we hoped once we got to Arles the mosquitoes would be far behind us.

Those first few kilometres were filled with relief. However the stress and the bites had taken their toll on us. We needed a rest day and we weren't getting one. We decided once we got through Arles which was about 30 kilometres away we would look for a place to stop, rest and camp. We didn't make it to Arles though before our first stop. We were tired and needed to change as it was turning out to be yet another lovely hot sunny day, although it was a lot windier. It was a successful stop, only one mosquito managed to find us. Wahoo! Things were looking up. We could also eat as I still had a little bit of food in my pannier from the day before. Feeling replenished we could finally sit down and laugh about the ordeal we had faced for the past

15 hours and how funny we must've looked. Sadly though the joke was most certainly on us. Our legs were now like patchwork, red blotches covered our bodies we looked like we had just stepped out of a Victorian sewer, totally diseased. There was no way we would find a hotel looking like this. We would definitely be rough camping today.

The roads were quiet and the sun was shining however a headwind can easily ruin your day however today it was welcomed because the wind helped keep the mosquitoes at bay. It was still hard going though.

Fortunately, after what seemed like ages, we made it out of the Camargue. We had escaped the mosquitoes narrowly but they had certainly left their mark. When we got to Arles we found out it was market day and very busy. We crossed over Le Rhône and into the heart of the city. We knew Arles had a rich roman history with the Barbegal aqueduct and mill. The Barbegal aqueduct was constructed to provide drinking water to Arles, all the way from the Alpille mountain chain. Arles has been an important city since then with it's position on the Rhône controlling large amounts of land. Arles although it has a population of just 50,000 covers an area seven times larger than Paris. It is amazing what weird facts stay with you once you leave a city.

Eventually we found what we were looking for, what we look for every morning, a boulangerie. Hallelujah! I collapsed down on the pavement outside, exhausted. Tom went in and came out with two huge baguettes and pain au chocolates, yes we were hungry. The woman inside the shop had asked Tom if he was alright and whether he needed a doctor, we obviously were looking terrible. The bite marks had swollen at this point to the size of 10 pence pieces. It was horrible. We agreed that we could punch the other person though if we caught them itching as we knew this would be bad. We just needed to recover and fast.

There was no point rushing breakfast, today was our rest day after all. However we thought that if we could end up doing 80 kilometres then we will have done a half day. Two half days would be better than one full rest day. At least that meant we only had another 40 or so kilometres left to cycle. There it was, another plan; we had become very good at making new plans. The sun was now getting higher and it was already 33°C at only 9:30, yet another hot day ahead.

We pedaled on for a short while, taking in the scenery and chilling. This was how the cycle was meant to be. However it was becoming blisteringly hot and we were suffering. We stopped for a break mid-morning in the shade. I needed to answer the call of nature so went about finding some bushes out of sight. It was nice doing it in the open in the sun. Well it was until I stood up and turned around. I looked at where I had been squatting and saw the biggest spider I had ever seen. It was sat on a web which was about two foot across. I jumped back in shock. Then I suddenly noticed more webs. It was like being in the film 8 legged freaks. My heart was now beating fast, I am not afraid of spiders. I think it was just my near escape and the feeling that they were crawling all over me that shook me. Now I could empathize with Tom about his snake incident yesterday. A couple of very close calls!

Returning to our usual obsession of food and water, we hadn't seen a supermarket in ages and in the hot summer heat we were running low on water. Yes we may have been in paradise, but we needed water and fast. We decided to ration our remaining fluids and pushed on to the next town hoping there would be a supermarket. We couldn't even knock on someone's door because there were no houses. We were between villages and surrounded by fields. Luckily there were trees lining the roads which gave us invaluable protection from the Mediterranean sun.

It almost seemed as if just as we escaped one evil we were presented with another one. Luckily eventually we managed to make it to a big Intermarché. We went in, bought a lot of food and plenty of ice tea. This was becoming the drink of the cycle. We got it at every available opportunity, it was so refreshing and the sugar was good. We parked the bikes up and sat inside a bus shelter for about an hour, eating, talking and relaxing. It was very peaceful. Now it was beginning to feel like a rest day. Finally.

Throughout the afternoon we took similar breaks from the heat. Finding shade, all the while looking for camping spots. We hadn't seen any! Everywhere was exposed and flat. Not perfect for wild camping. After passing through Saint-Martin-De-Crau we joined the D113. This was the straightest road we had cycled on. It ran parallel to the A54 motorway and was pretty quiet as all heavy traffic was on there. This was where we knew we would find somewhere to camp. All along the side of the road was a small but fast flowing canal about 1.5 metres across, this was the Canal de Langlade. Every so often there would be a small bridge over the canal to the area beyond. These were often gravel filled or barren and looked like where trucks were parked when the motorway was being built. However we knew if we found one with enough cover it would be perfect to camp in. Separated from the road by the canal and out of sight by some bushes, that was the area we were looking for.

Finally when the dusk was drawing close and the sky was turning purple we found our camping spot. We had seriously considered many others along the road and had cycled a long way down it. However we knew, well we didn't but we had faith, that if we persevered we would find a great place to camp. We did. It was lovely. We set the tent up with our bikes lying beyond it. Then we used a concrete slab as a bench and set about cooking some pasta.

Today had hardly been a rest day; we had finished cycling almost 100 kilometres. However it had been worth it, we had faith we would feel fresh tomorrow. To be honest it felt good to be somewhere without those blessed mosquitoes. We finished just above Marseille almost at Salon-De-Provence, a successful day. We were on our holidays now. Raising money for charity and having a good time.

We're Finally Getting Somewhere
Cycling Day 8
Salon-de-Provence to Vidauban

We woke to the sound of trickling water, from the Canal de Langlade, it was very peaceful. I had been very apprehensive camping less than a foot above the water. Luckily though we had no problems and both had a fantastic nights sleep. My earplugs had worked a charm again. They were turning out to be my best purchase of the trip.

We were feeling fantastic. We were still itching, and full of a cold, but we had cycled nearly 1000 kilometres, a significant milestone.

It was almost as if we had had a crystallizing moment in our sleep. We realized that we were living our dreams. We had been thinking about this part of the trip for months. Now we were doing it. So it was time to put everything else behind us and just enjoy what would unfold. It was a very refreshing new view on life. I enjoyed it. Everything almost seemed clearer; we could identify what didn't matter and what we needed to focus on. This was what we had needed from the beginning; however there was nothing we could do about that now. We would just live in the present, take it as it came and move on.

I could tell we were going to fly today. Although we hadn't really had a rest day our legs felt great. It was definitely what we needed. We were both itching, literally, to get back on the bikes and cycle. This was a good thought as well, at least after eight days we weren't bored of turning those pedals. Thinking back there was nothing that ever got boring about it. You are constantly in a changing environment, seeing new sights and experiencing new experiences. To be other than inspired by such a vibrant, ever-changing environment, and life enriching experience, cannot be possible.

After todays pedalling we would be a third of the way around Europe. Finally a sizable chunk gone. We had made the 'hopefully wise' decision of getting up early today. We knew we would be in for another baking hot day. This would mean it would be hard riding in the heat of the day, so if we started early and had an afternoon siesta we could maximize our riding efficiency and enjoyment. Realizing all these things and having a rough plan of what lay ahead felt good. We knew what we had to do; we knew what we were capable of. Now we just had to sit on the bike for seven hours and do it.

We were on the road by 6:45, the fastest start and by far the earliest. Although initially we were a little bit groggy, we soon found our rhythm. Continuing down the D113 it seemed this straight road would never end. Eventually though we made it to the bigger town of Salon-De-Provence. There was another huge downhill which we almost hit 70 kph on. Tom managed to go faster than I though because he had better gear ratios, well that's the excuse I use. A poor workman blames his tools and a poor cyclist blames his bike. Despite the early start within about twenty minutes we already had taken off almost all our layers as it was heating up fast. We loved the weather; I think the past few days would've been utterly miserable had it been raining. However things have to go wrong on a trip. Despite you wanting everything to go your way and be perfect, part of it has to go wrong or be hard otherwise what story can you tell? The more things that go wrong the more interesting the story. So in a way I am lucky that so many things did go wrong on our cycle as now I can share and reminisce our perils. However at the time I did not have this foresight and instead felt thoroughly hard done by. Was it worth all this suffering just to make a bit of money for charity?

It was a Sunday. In Europe that means one thing, everywhere is closed. We knew from the offset that it would be a big challenge to find food today. No wonder Europe is in a huge recession, no one is able to buy anything because the shops are all closed. However we spied signs to an Intermarché and decided to follow in the hope that it would be open for a few hours, and that it wasn't too far away. It is very dangerous following road signs in France, they are everywhere and they are totally misleading. Rather than tell you distances they say "McDonalds 2 minutes straight on", well they say that in French but you get my jest. Little do they mention that you need to be travelling at the speed of light to reach McDonalds within two minutes. We once had this where we saw signs for a McDonalds and thought two minutes we could get there by lunch, lunch being two hours away. We did not reach this McDonalds until near dinner time.

Anyway fortunately in this instance we were rewarded with a huge Intermarché. I had trusted the signs because there was also a symbol on my GPS indicating a supermarket. However with it being a Sunday it wasn't opening for another 20 minutes. We decided to wait for it to open because we did not want to run the risk of going hungry. It wasn't a good feeling waiting around with nothing to do, wasting the cooler hours of the morning. However we knew we had no choice. Finally it opened and we were rewarded for waiting. Fresh baguettes still hot to the touch were waiting inside, alongside pizzas and plenty of other tasty foods. I stocked up on a few mini pre-cooked pizzas and two baguettes with some cheese. I also bought some Ice-tea and some fruit juice to keep my vitamin C levels up. I thought it had been a successful shop and the new weight of my bike agreed with this. I got quite a shock when I realized we had been there for nearly an hour. We quickly finished off a baguette each then hit the road again.

You could tell the Tour de France was close-by because there was a huge amount of riders on the roads. I don't think we had ever seen so many cyclists until then. There were lots of clubs out and also lots of groups of elderly cyclists. This was the embarrassing part; they were all going faster than us. We got overtaken by one old man on his Bianchi three times! He found this very funny; we shall never live it down. Yes we may have much heavier bikes and also be carrying panniers but we had just cycled almost 1000 kilometres. You'd think we'd be getting good at it by now, rather than being overtaken by OAPs. I have never been overtaken in England by any cyclist when I am out on the roads. In fact I make it my task not to be. So it was an utterly humiliating experience for the both of us. They truly put us in our place, so congratulations monsieur you thwarted us.

We cycled all morning, stopping every 40 minutes as usual. It was beautiful cycling, the road quality was superb. We wound our way through the barrenness of southern France. At some points we could've been on the surface of Mars. I wasn't expecting the climate to be this dry. It reminded us of trekking through the Sahara desert in Morocco when we were 15. It seemed today everyone else had gone to the coast or stayed indoors as our roads were relatively empty. We weren't complaining though, as you probably know cycling is much more fun on peaceful roads.

As we neared lunchtime I happened to glance down at the GPS. I scrolled over to the odometer and noticed that we had travelled 999 kilometres since setting off in Bilbao. Boy did that feel like a world away now. I shouted up to Tom and he cycled next to me so we could both watch the clock tick over to 1000. It was a momentous occasion. We were a third of the way around Europe, time to crack open the champagne -well not quite. This was a big moment for us. It suddenly seemed as if we were completing all of our goals, making France, Reaching the Med, Reaching Saintes-Maries-De-La-Mer –although that may have been a mistake. You can't beat the feeling of achieving a goal you've strived hard to complete. We were alive with accomplishment. We only had another 3 kilometres and we would be stopping for lunch, so we decided to start looking for some shade.

Three kilometres later and almost on cue we found some shade. It was wondrous. We lay down a tarpaulin and sprawled across it, ready to dig into our lunch. It was way too hot now to cycle so we would have a nice long maybe two hour lunch then get back on the road. We only had 60 kilometres left to cycle so under three hours for that should be fine. After we had eaten we decided it was time for a nap. We talked for a bit and snoozed. Reminisced about back home, it felt so far away now. There could be no turning back. I think that was a reason we had began to feel better. In a couple of days we would reach Monaco and Italy then we would stop travelling east but turn north, homewards. Whereas before today we had been going southeast every day, getting further away. We were on the Mediterranean stint now, after that would be the Alps, which we were expecting would make or break us, then after the mountains the final push to Rotterdam across northern Europe.

It was a good lunch break. We actually enjoyed the break from the sun. At least there were no spiders or snakes today. We were a bit nervous about the end of the day, as we would be joining the DN7. We did not know what to expect with this road, it looked quite major, we just assumed it would be a cross between an N-road and a D-road. We were pretty much right. So nothing we couldn't cope with. It was relaxed cycling; it felt very flat however it was more rolling terrain. By the end of the day we had done a mile of ascent. We had been worried about water as we were running low. Luckily a petrol station answered our prayers, yet again. After we got that sorted and had cycled 160 kilometres we looked for a place to camp. We knew we were in a good area for it because it was very unpopulated.

The only problem was it was very open next to the railway and motorway.

Finally we found what looked to be a good place. We had been looking for about half an hour. It was down from the road behind a row of Poplar trees. We could pitch our tent in a barren looking field. It seemed very rocky and the earth was a dark crimson colour, dyed by the sun. However it looked great, the only problem was that there was a house looking directly over it. Not wanting them to call the cops on us we decided it would be best to set up camp once it got darker. Then we would be able to sleep uninterrupted.

Happy that we had found a suitable camping spot we got on our bikes and pedalled back up the road to a bus shelter. This small open brick hut looked good; we had even considered camping in it. However it seemed a bit too small for that. We set up the stove and began cooking some curry. It was very tasty and just what we needed. Good thing we were able to get some water at the petrol station otherwise we might've gone hungry.

We did get some odd looks from drivers. Who would blame them? Two dirty teenagers with heavily laden bikes sat in an old bus stop poking at a stove with half a spork each. We looked out of place. We didn't care though, we were on our adventure and we were loving it. We had had another great day; all we could do was hope our streak would continue.

As we waited for the rice to boil we looked ahead at the route on the small screen of the GPS. We were what looked to be about 70 kilometres from the coast at Cannes and then it would probably be another thirty to Nice. That was where we were going to go tomorrow. We had always wanted to stay in Nice. So we decided to find a Hostel there. I text my Dad back at home and he sent back two addresses that we could try. Failing that we could always go to a tourist office. It was just nice to have somewhere to head to in Nice. With it only being 100 kilometres we knew we normally do this by lunch so we thought if we left early we could make it there by mid morning. Then we could relax. There we go, we had another plan. We were going to make it to Nice, tomorrow!

We sat back and enjoyed our curry, Bilbao to Nice, "bloody hell that's an awful lot of cycling buddy." During this time the ants had come in their hundred's of thousands. A few days ago we were plagued by mosquitoes, now we were plagued by ants. They were after the bits of dropped rice; I guess we were messy eaters! The ants were everywhere. I had an idea, I am not proud of my idea, it was very cruel. Try putting yourself in our shoes though. We were tired, alone, and scarred from our experience with the mosquitoes. We decided to go with my plan. We would try and torch the ants. I turned on the camping stove and put it to a blue flame, like on a Bunsen burner at school. I then turned it upside down trying to set them on fire. What happened instead what the gas all rushed to the flame and a huge fireball leapt out of the stove almost engulfing my head as it rose to the ceiling of the bus shelter. It is true, karma exists and I was punished for my cruel intent towards the ants. Tom upon seeing this exploded into laughter, I can imagine it must've been hilarious to watch. I jumped back my heart racing and then joined in the laughter. How could I have been so stupid? Tom will never let me forget that moment in the bus shelter.

After the night's entertainment, we relaxed a bit more. Messaged loved ones and when the light was fading cycled the 200 metres to our camping spot. We quickly put up the tent; we were definitely becoming a dab hand at this camping malarkey. We lay back and relaxed. Tom hoping he wouldn't have to wake up that much during the night to re-inflate his Thermarest. He had taken the precaution of lying out his clothes underneath him to keep him as comfy as possible. With the wind rattling the tent all around us, it had become very blustery whilst putting the tent up; it almost blew away on a few occasions. We set the alarm for 4:30, yes 4:30, and went to sleep. Another wild night in the lives of the 17 year old English boys travelling around Europe, hardly your classic 'lads' holiday'.

"It's nice here"
Cycling Day 9
Vidauban to Nice

We knew the 4:30am start was going to be killer. We did not anticipate how bad though, it was so bad we rewarded ourselves with an extra half an hour in bed. If we had got up at 4:30 it would've been too dark to do anything. However by 5 am it still was dark but we had managed to trick our bodies into thinking they had had a lie in. We were up fast and on the road by 5:30. If we thought yesterdays start was early and fast today's was in a league of its own.

We had to use the lights on our bikes because it was so dark. However the benefit of starting this early meant it was nice and cool; the roads were empty. We were sure they would fill up later on as the Monday morning rush hour began and people flocked to the coast, just like we were doing. We had already passed through Vidauban and it was way too early for any shops to be open so we only really had one option, pedal hard. Our aim was Nice by mid morning. However we knew we would have to eat before that if we didn't want to starve, so we agreed we would stop for breakfast on the seafront when we got there in Cannes. The first few miles were very fast, fuelled by excitement to reach the French Riviera. We flew past fields, all the while noticing that it was getting slightly hillier and slightly more built up. The harder cycling was good, it was what we needed to wake our legs up and stop us yawning.

It has been proven that we are actually at our happiest when we are anticipating something exciting, rather than us being happiest while we are doing that something. I can certainly vouch for this, as we couldn't wait to reach Nice. This was the 'destination' of the trip if ever there was one. Yes our journey was mainly a loop going through many different places however up to Nice we were going away and after Nice we were heading home. This in a sense made Nice the turning point of our trip. We were reaching a major city, for the first time, the next one after this would be Turin and then Geneva.

The more we cycled the busier the roads got. We followed the DN7 all the way to Fréjus and we made amazing time. Rather than heading to the coast straight away we took the fastest route to Cannes. This meant following the DN7 and beginning the climbing. We could almost smell the coast and thought it would all be down hill and flat from here on in. We couldn't have been more wrong. Slowly the gradient increased and we found ourselves in a mountainous region because the road kept climbing up and up. We began to think we had already entered the Alps. The roads twisted and turned their way up the hillside and we saw plenty of other cyclists. The low amount of cars was good, however the climbing was hard. The day was getting hot now, as it was already 9 am. We could feel it. We just kept thinking to ourselves, what goes up must come down; especially if we were going to the coast. However the road was still climbing through the barren rocks. It really did look like a Mars landscape now, but oddly beautiful. We tried to see it as practice for the Alps, which would begin soon. These were the first proper climbs we had had to do since the first couple of days in Spain. It was a shock to the system. However the previous 1000 kilometres in our legs had weathered and trained them, they were ready. We were fit. We were rested. We were going to make it over to the Mediterranean on the other side.

Finally after what had felt like hours of pedalling, in our lowest gears, we reached the top. It had been hard but the challenge had been good, now for a nice long descent, we hoped. This was the part I was slightly nervous about. I had managed since day one without a back brake. However this would be the first test on a proper mountain descent. Also the starts of things to come in the Alps. If I couldn't stop now the Alps would be very difficult and dangerous. I decided there was nothing I could do though; I would just have to go for it. Tentatively I rode over the crest of the hill behind Tom and began the descent.

It was fast, sharp, and exhilarating. We wound our way down the mountain, this side was much greener and we welcomed the shade. The shade combined with the lovely breeze we now had actually gave us goose bumps on the hot day. We weren't complaining though it felt amazing to be cool. Our make shift air-conditioning was working its charm. I had a couple of close encounters but after a while worked out what speed I needed to be going in the corners so that my singular brake could cope. On a normal bike you should be fine with just one brake, however with the added weight of two massive panniers this gave the bike a lot more inertia, making it much harder to stop. Now I just had to prey that my brake pads would last the next 1000 kilometres through the Alps. We flew down the hill, just managing not to lose control and before we knew it we were at the bottom and only a couple of kilometres from the sea front.

The sea air was rich in our nostrils willing us to push on. We were very hungry now and couldn't wait to find somewhere for breakfast. We arrived at the coast at San Peyre. This was how we had imagined it. The French Riviera. The sea was glistening and sparkling in the morning sun, which was now getting pretty high in the sky. The coast and beach stretched as far as the eye could see, with the road running right on top of it. That was where we were cycling. About twenty metres from the sea we pedalled along the purpose built bike paths. Smooth asphalt and a clear path, that was the life. It was great. We soon managed to find someone to take our picture in front of the sea. Not long after that we were sprawled back on deck chairs over looking the beach. We had found breakfast.

It was now nearly 10 am and we had already cycled 75 kilometres, pretty good if you ask me. We had also managed to find the best pain au chocolates in France. They were fresh, they were tasty, they were chocolaty; they were delicious. I had six of them; even the owners of the shop were impressed. The intake of sugar was definitely what I needed; I had felt on my last reserves. The pain au chocolates revived me and put me in a ready and raring mood to reach Nice. We sat relaxing for about half an hour, basking in the shade and delight of reaching Cannes. We then decided we should cycle the last hour and a bit to Nice and the hostel.

This was a new part of France for Tom and I; we had never been here before. We couldn't help feel it didn't feel like France at all. The luxury hotels, posh cars, and golden sands. This was a completely different France to the one we had been cycling through for the past week. I liked the change although I wasn't sure which type of France I preferred. I think the quieter farm village side of France was nicer to cycle through; it was more peaceful and felt more genuine. However the new France had everything we 'needed', the beach and the sea. We pedalled further down the coast, going past the cinemas of central Cannes. Most of the time we were on bike paths, which were fantastic. They were well maintained, free of other traffic and most importantly free of walkers. That's the last thing you want, someone to step out in front of you, because it's a sure fire way to get you both injured.

As we moved out of Cannes Tom tried to teach me how to cycle without using my hands. I had never tried this before so was a little nervous about going for it. Tom on the other hand is a natural; he probably cycles more without hands than with them. It turns out it is actually much easier than it looks. Just sit up tall, hold your core and pump your legs. However one tip; remember you don't have your hands on because if a pothole comes up it is hard to ride over it when you have no hands on your handlebars. We refrained from trying wheelies because all the weight over the back of our bikes made them nigh impossible.

Flat, sunny and smooth. That would be how I would describe the idyllic cycling along the French promenade. It was wondrous. We knew we were going to make Nice in great time; the early start was beginning to seem worth it now. However looking at the map, the address of the hostel looked very far away from the beach. We decided we might as well go and have a look because allegedly it had good reviews and wasn't too expensive. It was absolutely sweltering now, extremely sticky cycling conditions. I don't think the sea had ever looked more inviting. We knew once we had checked in we would head straight for the beach. Finally after about 20 kilometres of cycling we reached the heart of Nice. It was very nice.

We cycled up and down the coast for a while, exploring and taking pictures, it was very relaxed. The sea looked amazing, part of us wanted to just leave our bikes, jump in the sea and spend two weeks here then get a plane home. It was so tempting. We resisted that temptation, for now, and headed in land and up-hill towards the 'Villa St. Exupery Gardens Hostel' at 22 Avenue Gravier. If you type that into a map you will see our predicament. It is about 6 kilometres from the beach up a huge hill. Wahoo. Nice looked like a maze of small side streets and one-way systems so I decided to try out the navigating function on my Garmin GPS. I set it to find routes for cycling, and boy did it do that. It was amazing. It knew every road, which you would hope, but more impressively it used every road. We were heading down alleyways, one-way streets all the while cutting up the hill, evading the traffic. It was superb, all the way it worked we were never lost and it told us where to go on junctions. It really saved us here, there was no way we would have ever managed to navigate our way 6 kilometres inland by ourselves. Eventually we made it to

Avenue Gravier which is a turning off the steepest road ever built. I kid you not. We had cycled and walked up some steep roads. However this was a near cliff face. We tried cycling and failed. Our bikes almost flipped over because of the gradient and all the weight over the back wheels. There was no way we could cycle up this road. Slowly we climbed up, pushing down on our handlebars to balance the bikes. We had made it.

Down a gravel path, plants overhanging all around the hostel emerged before us like a beacon of hope. Now the moment of truth. Would they have any beds available? We parked the bikes and went up to the front desks with our biggest smiles on, trying not to look that sweaty. We were received with an equally warm smile and told that they had no beds in dorms left, our hearts sunk. She must've seen this on our faces so she replied that they did have a private twin room free for the night but it was 90€. We beamed and gladly accepted this offer. 45€ each was our price limit and at least then we could relax. Unfortunately check in wasn't till 2 pm. We had no worries about this; we would just go to the beach! The hostel workers were great; there was a special locked room for luggage and a separate one for bikes. Rather embarrassingly we locked our dilapidated tired looking bikes next to some much more expensive enviable Bianchi's and retreated to go and get changed into beach clothes. We had each brought some 'normal' clothes with us in our panniers for instances like this. However I only had tight swimming shorts, which were much smaller than I remembered when I packed them. I decided it would be pretty indecent of me to walk around in these so put a pair of regular shorts on over the top, for the long walk down to the sea. It was a holiday now. Over 100 kilometres cycled, not yet noon and we were heading down to the beach.

We walked down into Nice with an Aussie tri-athlete we had met at the Hostel called Aaron. He was a great guy, looked the spit of Lance Armstrong as well. He had just finished his 'Tri-season' and was having a break in Nice after it. Unfortunately he had left his "sunnies" on the plane so was suffering a bit. He was looking for somewhere to eat so once we made it to central Nice he parted with a "See you later mates" which I reciprocated in the same accent, feeling like a massive fool. I don't know why I do it, I can just pick up accents really quickly and always end up copying peoples accents. Hoping that he either hadn't heard or didn't think I was taking the piss, which I wasn't, we walked further down the hill.

We had no idea where we were going but were under the general impression that if we proceeded to walk downhill then we would eventually be in the sea. Sound logic and it worked. After what seemed like no time at all we were lying back on the pebbles 'sur la plage'. I had stripped down to my tiny swim shorts; they didn't look so silly now. However I was aware of how small they were so decided to brave it and jump into the sea. I dived in and was shocked by how cold the water was. It was freezing, almost on Britain's standards. It was refreshing though and I loved it. It was what our muscles needed, what our slowly healing bites needed and it was what our heads needed. Tom was keen to get in the water too, however after seeing my shock on how cold it was, he was a tad more nervous getting in. Tip toeing from rock to rock, jumping about like a little girl he slowly edged his way closer to the water. He then began the slow process of gradually edging further in. Eventually he immersed himself in the Med. As we swam around it felt like we were cleansed of all the bad things that had happened to us. We would move on with a fresh start from now invigorated and optimistic that no more bad things would happen. If you can believe that you're as mad as we were. Of course we were going to have plenty more problems. However we realised now that they were all part of our adventure.

We spent a good few hours on the beach and in the sea. It was great and so relaxing. Afterward we walked slowly back up through Nice, finding postcards to send home and exploring the city. There was lovely architecture and lots of smiling faces. As we neared the hostel we saw what looked like a nice Italian restaurant and decided we would have dinner there later. When we got to the hostel and found our room it was great! We were on the top floor with a huge balcony, en-suite and largish bedroom. I had a shower to wash all the salt off me and Tom collapsed onto the bed exhausted and quickly snored his way into a calm oblivion.

I had a refreshing long shower then lay on my bed and skyped my girlfriend, Alice. It was great being able to see her however it made me miss her, and home, a lot. I couldn't wait till the day I got home and could see everyone again. Though I quickly sent those thoughts to the back of my head. It is dangerous thinking of the end when we weren't even past half way. It was good being able to see the Just Giving page and see that we had raised about £1500 and more money was rolling in every day. We were roughly raising a pound a kilometre for the MS Society. This was good as it gave what we were doing a sense of purpose and beneficence.

At 6 Tom finally woke from his nap, still exhausted. It was his turn for a shower now. Somehow in the process he managed to flood the whole of the room. We used up all the towels trying to dry it. No showers in the morning! After we got ready we were starving so headed down to the Italian we had spied earlier in the day. The waitress didn't speak English, only French, so we did have our work cut out. Especially when it came to explaining that we would like another portion of mains. Tom ate a huge burger and chips, then a pizza. I settled for two pizzas. However the final slice beat me. It had all sunk to my stomach and I was feeling very ill. Fortunately Tom had no problems polishing it off for me.

It was a great meal. A super end to the best day yet. It had been amazing, felt like a day off yet we had still covered long miles. Unfortunately the 4:30am start had killed us so we could not accept requests to go out for drinks. Instead we were sensible and in bed by 9:30pm. Needless to say, it did not take us long to drift off.

The Accident
Cycling Day 10
Nice to Fontan

The sun drifted through the gaps in the blinds and we woke up very relaxed. Today was going to be another half day so there was no sense in rushing. We had paid for breakfast in the hostel so we were going to get the most out of it. We lazily got dressed and headed downstairs where we met Aaron again and walked into the dining room. Breakfast was great. I still wasn't feeling a hundred percent so couldn't eat as much as I would've liked but Tom cleaned up well. He had many bowls of cereal and countless pieces of toast. It was great. The orange juice was refreshing and made us feel good about what lay ahead today.

Our aim today was to do about 80-100 kilometres and cycle through three countries: France, Monaco and Italy. This was big for us; it gave the feeling of real progress crossing borders. Today we would cross four borders. We also couldn't wait to visit Monaco and have a look around because neither of us had been before.

After breakfast, we had been eating for a good hour; we headed back up to the room to pack. Tom was craving a shower; needless to say the room once again flooded. Luckily this time nothing was on the floor so we managed to keep everything dry. We began the process of totally repacking our panniers. This meant it was time for new cycling clothes and more importantly new socks! Mmm the feel of fresh cotton socks. It was unbeatable at that point. We felt clean and fresh. Worryingly that feeling went away surprisingly quickly. We guiltily left the pool of water on the floor and went downstairs to collect our bikes. We said our goodbyes and thanks, and then hopped on for what we hoped would be a fun day in the saddle.

Funnily enough, cycling down the really steep road was a lot more fun than getting up it had been the previous day. Rather than follow GPS instructions we decided to make our way to the sea front the same way we had done on foot. We would just go downhill. When we walked we had followed the tramlines almost the whole way, we had also seen plenty of cyclists, so decided this would be a good route to take. It was. We cycled through the heart of Nice as we bid farewell to this vibrant and lovely city.

Just like that my wheel became jammed. I had foolishly got it stuck between the tram tracks. It was in a rut and so was I. I had been travelling over 30 kph down the hill and Tom was to the side of me. Well he was. Not anymore. I came crashing down. As I flew from my saddle the worst happened. A tram pulled out of the station about 20 metres away and was heading straight for me. It was an instinct. As I came crashing down I curled up into a ball. I feared the worst and could feel my heart trying to jump out of my chest. As I came crashing down onto the cobbles I heard an almighty crack. I was in a ball now and the tram was on top of me. It was not going to stop. I tried to roll away. I was cemented still. The tram continued to move; it had missed my head by about an inch. That was too close.

I looked down at my bike. However I was distracted by the dark red fluid covering my legs. It was sticky in the late morning heat and formed a sharp contrast with the light stone ground onto which it dropped. Where was all this blood coming from? Then I saw my knee, yes my actual knee. The white bone was protruding from a deep cut in my leg. Afraid I would pass out from this sight I quickly put my hand down to cover the patella in blood and shroud it from view. By now we were centre of attention in the area. I was well aware that I was still lying on the tram tracks and was now beginning to think rationally. At the moment I was in the hot sun with people all around. I needed to move to a quieter place in the shade.

Tom and I moved through the crowds, grabbing our bikes and other items which had fallen off during the crash, to under an archway. It was here where I could get out my first aid kit and fix the wound. Apart from a few cuts on my legs, shoulder and my knee I was unhurt. However my knee needed serious attention. It wasn't a huge cut but it was deep to the bone, as if all the flesh had been gouged out by the metal ruts of the tram tracks. I got out some alcoholic wipes to clean the wound. This was going to sting. I braced myself, and then went in. It had to be done I knew it. I rubbed and scraped at the wound trying to clean it and get all the dirt out. It just would not stop bleeding. Tom went about gathering all my things. Luckily the snapping sound when I fell had been one of my panniers and not a bone. Despite some scrapes it seemed nothing was damaged. Apart from my bike 'Samantha' her handlebars were scraped and torn. The tape on the handle bars had disintegrated and the brake hoods were thoroughly bent out of shape. She was in a bad way.

Eventually, many blood soaked wipes later, I thought I had cleaned the wound sufficiently. I then tried to use a spray on plaster, this stung like a b*tch. I was not being a wimp about it either, that really hurt. It also was totally useless because the wound was far too deep for it to have any effect. I decided I would have to put a pad on the wound then apply a bandage around that really tight. My reasoning was that this would apply pressure to the wound and reduce blood flow. I could barely walk. How on earth was I meant to cycle? Let alone cycle 2000 more kilometres. I couldn't think like this though, I had learnt that by now. I just had to try, focus on today, and take it as it comes.

I am sure many of you are asking yourselves, why didn't I just go to the hospital? Well passers by and the police who came over to check if I was okay suggested it. However I knew I couldn't have stitches, how was I meant to cycle then? It would be a failure. I couldn't let that happen. It was really painful however I felt that I had to go on, hopefully the pain in my knee would distract me from the lactate build up in my legs. If I had gone to the hospital we would have definitely lost one day, it would have been expensive and most likely that would be the end. If we carried on for another couple of weeks I could get it checked out when I got back to the UK. As long as I kept it bandaged and clean it would be fine, surely?

That was my mentality at the time of the accident. Looking back now I think it would have been a good idea to get it checked out even if I did refuse the treatment. They would have at least cleaned it well and dressed it properly. Maybe it wouldn't have got infected and I wouldn't have been left with a huge lump of a scar on my left knee. Hindsight is a wonderful thing. Unfortunately I didn't have it. So I am now left with a permanent memento of that day.

After securing a bandage onto my leg and repairing Samantha we were 'ready' to start cycling again. I was feeling very delicate and uneasy. I really did not want to do big miles today; thank god it was only a half-day. Fortunately the pain I had when trying to walk was not reciprocated when cycling. I had very little pain when trying to cycle. Thank god! Maybe I will be able to do big miles with this injury, I thought. Finally we reached the coast at Nice and joined our route once more. We bumped into an avid photographer and we got him to take our photograph. One of the best ones of us from the trip! I sent it through to my mum who could then upload it onto the Just Giving website, updating people on our progress. However of course she scrutinised it and noticed the bandage! Fortunately I played it down via an exchange of texts and it was good to hear from her.

I loaded up on ibuprofen, it kicked in and my leg was hurting less than it was originally, heading in the right direction of recovery at least.

We curved round the winding, busy, roads of the French Riviera heading for Monaco. It was only about 20 kilometres so we would make it in under an hour. An hour of riding under the baking sun later, being constantly overtaken by expensive super-cars, we were there. We entered the sovereign city state of Monaco. Entering Monaco was like going into an exclusive party. Everywhere you looked there was another flamboyant parade of wealth, be it a car, a boat, or a house. Everyone, bar the tourists, was rolling in it. However with all the tourists it did have a more down to earth feel. We liked this; at least not everyone here was looking down at us. Then again, we were two English, lycra-clad, sweaty teenagers, anyone in their right minds should've looked down at us. Yes by now my once clean clothes in the morning were splattered with dirt, sweat and blood. Wondrous.

Not surprisingly we didn't know our way round Monaco. Instead we pedalled around for a bit, and then we decided to follow our trick of heading downhill until we reached the harbour. Wow! I finally understood the wealth of Monaco.

Once in the Harbour we decided we needed lunch, this was a tricky one. There was no chance we would be able to find reasonably priced food. Being on a budget we decided our best bet was a supermarket. Our wallets still got a thumping, everything was over twice what we would pay for it normally and this was a supermarket we normally went in to as well! Oh well, needs must.

After we had feasted on our expensive lunch out. We decided to pedal round a bit more and try to find the Palace. After getting lost, because someone gave us bad directions not because we couldn't execute them, we reached the steps leading up. Yes steps. These were huge steps as well, I just knew it would be nigh impossible for me to get up with my knee how it was and carrying a heavily laden Samantha. Tom was keen though and I'm really glad he pushed me to doing it. It was hard, sweaty (need I say it), work. Heaving the bikes up each step. We got to a flat part and Tom scouted ahead to see how much further we would have to climb.

"Not far" he reported back, so we went for the summit. Once at the top it was refreshing, a sea breeze cooled us off nicely. We entered the old quadrangle, wheeling our bikes; it was very pretty just what you'd expect from a building built in 1191. However it did not look this old at all, it had clearly been renovated since then. It turned out that the palace was renovated by Honoré V in 1841 and these renovations continued through out the 19th century. The Grimaldi family has ruled Monaco and lived in the Prince's Palace since 1297. However we were unable to enjoy the Palace for long because after we had had our pictures taken we were kindly asked to leave and take our bikes with us. Apparently they were an obstruction, even though we were wheeling them about and it wasn't that busy. We left. However we managed to find a road to cycle down, if only we had found this on the way up. It was a lovely road back down to the port curving around the many buildings of the palace.

Once back down it was approaching 2pm so we decided we had better head on and keep cycling. On our way out of Monaco we cycled through the infamous Monte-Carlo and posted our postcards home from a post office there. Once back in France we were only a few more kilometres of French Riviera away from our fourth country, Italy. Those final few kilometres of France were very sedate and relaxed. There was little traffic on the roads because the motorway was so close. Just like that we were in Italy. A few metres and a whole different language, one that we did not know. These few days would be interesting.

Once across the border we pulled over above a stony beach in the shade where we drank our "12 fruits multivitamin fruit juice", it was fruity. The water was glistening and completely clear. It was hot, as usual, but we were learning to cope with it. Slowly our bodies were adapting to life on the road. We got talking to a delightful Australian couple that were doing a road trip of Europe and had already been around the UK. It was great speaking to them and about the forthcoming London Olympics. They were hoping to be back in Australia by then though; we would still be on the road for the opening ceremony. They were heading a similar route to us as well. Although covering it significantly faster. They were hoping to get to Turin tonight or early tomorrow whereas it would be the day after next for us, hopefully. They were lovely and it was only when they got up to leave that we realised that the lady was blind. That got us thinking, it would be so terrible to be blind and not see all this wonder. To miss out on the amazing views we had seen and experienced is something we both found quite hard to imagine. We immediately felt in awe of the woman and we hoped that they both had a fantastic end to their trip.

It was time for Italy and time for the tunnels. It was time to get cycling again. That was the reason we pulled over initially after crossing, there was a huge tunnel. Our last experience of tunnels was in Spain, which was an experience neither of us wanted to repeat, so you can understand our hesitation on entering one. These tunnels were fantastic though, fully lit, it was like cycling in daylight. The Italian drivers were surprisingly fantastic too and always gave us plenty of room, we weren't expecting this. We would follow the SS1 to Ventimiglia where we would then turn off the Med and head north, finally, on the SR20. The next time we would be at the coast now would be when we reached the Ferry at Rotterdam. This road would eventually lead back into France, although in the direction of Turin, we would enter Italy again after a brief stint in France. Our aim for the day had been to reach France, again, even with all the breaks and my knee we were still on course for this, so we felt good. There was very little in this region of Italy that we saw, the road seemed to be the only major thing. However it was still very quiet which made the cycling a dream. Also with the many tunnels it meant we could hear cars and trucks coming a heck of a long way off. The Alps were definitely beginning now, the mountains were getting bigger and the tunnels were getting longer. We cycled through a tunnel that was 2430 metres long! It seemed to go on and on when we were on our bikes. We just kept hoping the Italians had drilled through every mountain and we wouldn't have to do any climbing. A fact we knew was never going to be true. However it was a bit unnerving that we had almost had enough of climbing and the Alps had barely even started.

Finally we made it back into France just as the light was fading. Now we had to begin the task of finding a place to wild camp. It felt like days since we had last camped, however that was probably because so much had happened over the past 36 hours. We neared the town of Breil-Sur-Roya and saw a magnificent sight. It was the perfect village, a tranquil lake, old buildings, fishermen; all shrouded in mountains. Wow! We were taken a back; this was by far the most beautiful town we had cycled through.

Even better it had a Spar so we could get some food. We cycled on a bit further to cook up some pasta. Once again the ants were out to join in our meal. We were struggling to find a camping spot because everywhere was too steep, unless it was on the road. We had gone past a couple of cheap campsites which looked okay but we were still scarred from our Saintes-Maries experience so persevered, determined to rough camp.

It was now getting very dark and fast, the sun had disappeared behind the mountain tops long ago. We were still cycling. We had not lost faith yet though; we had managed to find a spot every day before so we wouldn't fail today. Finally when we thought everything was lost the land opened up on our right next to the river La Roya. This was it. Just out of sight from the road as it was lower down; flattish and perfect. Just fingers crossed no flash floods. We cleared the area of bracken then put the tent up quickly. We took advantage of having fresh mountain water running so closely and washed our socks and feet, it was freezing! Although very refreshing, I made a mental note to remember to wash my face in it again in the morning. Feeling rested and after having re-dressed my wound we lay back after a very tiring rest day. It had been good though. Tomorrow the real climbing would begin.

The Collision
Cycling Day 11
Fontan to Carmagnola

Fortunately there were no flash floods during the night and we slept 'comfortably'. I should probably explain comfortably means Tom waking up every couple of hours to re-inflate his sleeping mat and me tossing and turning to relive pressure on my knee. However we felt rested and ready. Today we would be tested. Hopefully we would not be broken. We knew that we would have a great deal of climbing right from the off. Sensing this we were a little lethargic to jump onto our bikes and get pedalling. Eventually though we shook the tent of ants and were on our way.

Almost immediately my knee started seeping blood again. The constant movement combined with how deep the gash was meant it just wasn't healing. The slowest of deaths I thought to myself. Maybe I would bleed to death before the roads began to wind, and then at least I wouldn't have to climb. A weird sort of lose-lose situation, I either do the climbs and don't die or die and then I won't have to do the climbs. Weirdly or worryingly, this worked in motivating me. Distracting me from the task at hand. Being on a cycle-tour is an odd way of living. You can't fully concentrate on the cycling; you would go insane from the pressure, tiredness and loneliness. However you can't forget about it. You therefore find yourself in a peculiar state of play, on the one hand you must focus on the cycling, the road, what lies ahead in order to ensure nothing goes wrong. However on the other hand your brain is fighting you, always telling you to have a breather, looking around for distractions, finding niggling pains in body parts you didn't even know you had. I believe this is why our minds are so delicate when we are on tour. You can be in a great mood, then in a brief second a car can overtake you too close and plunge your thoughts into darkness. I am a victim of this, my mind was whirring away with worry and that is why I was glad I had Tom. Tom never let anything bother him; he always had a cheeky grin on his face and made it his job to make me laugh. Not a hard task seeing as Tom's uncanny wit and quick thinking meant he would rival many stand-ups. He knew how to make me smile and lift me from the dark thoughts that we both experienced continuously. Beginning the pedalling for that day, as with everyday, I just hoped our moods would stay good. Although knowing it would be hard as no doubt these mountains would tire us, we would just have to take it as it came.

Those first few kilometres were good, all uphill we saw them as good practice for what lay ahead and a good warm up. We had no idea how high or for how far we would have to climb. All we did know was that in about 25 kilometres the roads got awfully windy. We were following the river Roya all the way up the D6204, probably to its' source. The roads were totally empty and it was lovely peaceful cycling. We curved around with the river; amazed at the huge path it had carved for itself into the rock face.

All along there were signs of its immense power, huge boulders and deep crevasses all hewn away by it. We leapfrogged with a French couple all the way up; they eventually got the edge on us when we stopped at the tiny village of Tende for some breakfast.

I took our stop to carefully redress my wound before the proper climbing started. I decided to put on an even tighter bandage to see if applying a lot of pressure would be more beneficial. Tom, on the other hand, decided he was very hungry and came out of the local shop armed with 120, yes 120, biscotti biscuits. Apparently they were on offer and because everything else was so expensive in there he thought this was a good decision. Now I like biscuits as much as the next guy but even I knew eating 120 without a cup of tea you'd be sure to get a serious dry mouth. Tom was not fazed though and was up for the challenge. So there we were sat on some steps outside the post office/ general store with 120 biscuits and 2 baguettes. Talk about carbohydrate loading. We knew we would be needing the energy!

Food digesting we were psyched up for what lay ahead; actually we were pretty nervous. It would be our first proper climb. It's time to begin the mountains. The road was near vertical, well it felt like that. Winding and winding, we were inching our heavy-laden bikes up the mountain. We were now on the Col de Tende, we were hurting. Sweat was trickling down my brow into my eyes and they were stinging, although this had the benefit of shrouding my vision from the road ahead. I could not see what perils lay ahead me. Tom had taken the lead, naturally, as he was by far the better climber and the more athletic. I was out of my seat the whole way up as it was easier on my knee, I paid the price though, and it hurt a lot. My once clean clothes were now a sodden, salty, sweaty mess. Dust from the road was sticking to my perspiring skin, making me appear more tanned than I actually was. However after almost two weeks outside we were both boasting impressive tan lines.

Finally after what had been the hardest climb of my life we reached the top and the Italian border. My legs felt like they were about to fall off. We looked back down into the valley, shocked at how far we had come. I looked at the GPS and it said we were standing at 1777 metres above sea level, by far the highest we had ever cycled. The air was noticeably thinner, and so were we after that climb. Our lungs strained to replenish our oxygen deficit and get rid of the lactate that had built up in our bodies. We were spent. Hopefully that would be it for the climbing. It was now 11 and getting, not surprisingly, very hot. When we reached the top we were met with a peculiar sight. Not a hill top finish but a tunnel. Up to this point we had really liked the Italian tunnels they were all extremely well lit and were safe to cycle through. However this one boasted no cycling signs on its entrance, oh no! We decided it couldn't be that far so we would just sprint through it. It was our only option, we could not turn back, there was no other way! However we could not just cycle through, there was only one lane so the tunnel operated via traffic lights letting traffic through from opposite sides of the mountain alternately. This was going to make it quite difficult; we didn't want to get hit on by a truck coming the opposite direction because we were too slow getting through. We were stuck.

Luckily Antonio answered our prayers. He ran up to us from the long line of cars waiting to go through the tunnel and told us what we knew, it was not possible to cycle through. We asked him if there was another way, he pointed back down the mountain and then pointed up, signalling that there was another, steeper road, which passed over the top. We tried to convey that this was not an option. We were dead from the cycling, the possibility of going back down to only go back up again was not an option. We tried to thank him but told him we were just going to cycle through the tunnel. He then motioned us to follow him. Intrigued, and not with much of an option, we followed. He was running and shouted us to hurry; with confused looks on our faces we reached his pickup truck. He moved about some stuff in the back and then told us to lift our bikes into the back of it. What a nice gesture. Tom and I quickly conversed and decided to take Antonio up on his kind offer. We hoisted up the bikes into the truck and not a moment too soon. The lights had gone green. Antonio could not afford to wait around and needed to make this set of lights. He guided me forward to the car in front and put me in a couple's back seat. Tom jumped into his passenger seat and we were off.

Yes, it was that hasty. One moment we were toying up our options, next I was speeding through the Tunnel du Col de Tende. It seemed Antonio had spoken to this elderly Italian couple before opening up their back door and putting me in. They were delightful, however there certainly was a language barrier. I managed to convey that

I was from England and heading towards Turin and that was pretty much it. They seemed to find it very interesting and fun though. I just loved sitting down on a comfy leather seat in a luxury car, such simple pleasures already seemed so exotic and invigorating. However I was distinctly aware of my dirtiness and smell, I was immediately embarrassed and in a way couldn't wait to get out of the car. It felt wrong. I felt bad for intruding on these peoples lives; they definitely didn't know what they were signing up for when they agreed to take me across the border. They probably had to disinfect my seat after I got out, I certainly would have. They were lovely though; I was genuinely touched by this show of affection and help from these Italians. Going out of their way to help us. There was no way we would have been able to cycle it, because it turned out the tunnel was about 5 kilometres long. And that meant we had 5 kilometres less to cycle today in order to make it to the outskirts of Turin.

We reached the end of the tunnel and were bathed in the warm sunlight once again. I expressed my thanks with many "Grazies" and bid farewell to the kind couple. Immediately I wished to be out of the thirty-degree heat and back into a nicely air-conditioned car. After a short while Tom and Antonio turned up, being the last car to make it through. Phew. During the journey Tom had been speaking on the phone to Antonio's son, who was translating everything back to Antonio about our trip and what we were doing. He was very impressed, but not as impressed as we were of him. He was a lovely man and there needs to be more people like him in the world. We hoisted our bikes off his pickup and bid farewell. We stood there in awe of the Italian people's warmth and generosity. We were on a high. We just could not believe our luck.

The day continued to get warmer, only now we were on a lovely long descent so welcomed a lovely cool breeze. We dropped down the mountain, following rivers, through forests and past fields. The roads were silent; when we did come across a car they rewarded us by giving us loads of room and a friendly toot of the horn. This was the cycle tour I had envisaged all those months ago.

When we were choosing a route, planning out every minute detail, there wasn't much point. Expect the unexpected. Everything had happened to us so far, and the only thing that had stayed constant was the route. We had suffered hardships, when the whole expedition hung in the balance. Yet we were still pedalling away and still having fun. It is very easy to focus on the negatives while you are riding along; the voices in your head begin to talk you down. However I think Tom and I made a good pair we always could read how the other person was feeling and how to treat them. Whether to start up yet another conversation about Lord of the Rings or Top Gear or just break into song. We were used to the hard times now we knew how to deal with them and with each other. We felt invincible. Nothing could stop us now. We had conquered our first huge climb and were still pedalling the other side. We had over come colds, plague by mosquitoes, a huge gash in my knee, getting lost, searching for camp spots and countless other tasks. Dealing with these was all second nature by now. We had adapted to life on the road. We had become at one with our bikes and of the environment around us. We were loving it.

We had just completed the descent and were pedalling across a long flat stretch of road which just had the occasional big truck on. Smiles were fixed on our faces. Basking in the midday sun, Tom decided to pull alongside me. Upon noticing a truck in the distance Tom began to filter behind me, something felt weird, so I looked around.

"You alright?" I asked Tom.

"Yeah" He replied.

I turned back; the truck was bearing down on us now. Something was definitely wrong, my bike felt weird. Then our world came crashing down.

Next thing I knew I was lying on my side in the middle of the road. Sensing danger I immediately got up and wheeled my bike to the side of the road. I shouted at Tom to get up. I was angry, this was totally his fault. I grabbed my panniers, which had fallen off in the impact, and other equipment, which was littering the road. Then I shouted at Tom again. There were cars coming he needed to move. Luckily he had responded and had begun moving his things to the side as well. My body ached, luckily though I hadn't fallen on my left knee but the other side. However that meant that my right side was now cut up, bruised and bleeding. Luckily we managed to get everything out of the road before any cars came. Then we began the painful process of assessing the damage. I looked down at my bike and was immediately pissed with Tom. All the handlebar tape and bar was shredded, my brakes were bent and there were scrapes to the frame. Tom on the other hand appeared to not have much wrong at all. I felt this was unfair because in my mind it had been him who had caused the accident. I was deliberately short with him because I wanted him to know that I was angry. For the second day in a row I had come off my bike and was injured, only this time so was my bike. I spent a good 15 minutes re packing my bike and adjusting it, there was nothing I could do for the bar tape.

We pushed off in silence. The heat of the day only worsened our feelings. We were back on a low. I just wanted to find somewhere to eat so we could move on. Shrouded in my own thoughts I just kept on pedalling. It was a good while before I looked behind and saw that Tom wasn't there. Yes, this day just got worse. I turned my bike around and set off the way I had come in search of Tom. This was frustrating, now we were losing time because of him, as well as the crash.

Then I spotted him in the distance. It was clear his bike was in a bad way too. When I got to him I realised his front brake had broken. Immediately I felt bad, I had been too callous, too rash. Of course he hadn't meant to cause the crash; it was an accident after all. We agreed that this was not a suitable place to stop, so pedalled on to the outskirts of Cuneo.

Tom shouted up to me. He had had enough. We pulled in at a car park with no shade. The sun was boiling our blood by this time. Tom threw his bike on the ground saying it was unfixable and unrideable. He then said he would just get a train home. He tossed his helmet to the ground and left.

So, I thought, this is it. This is how far we had come and how far we would get. It had been a long 11 days and very tiring at that. We had a lot to look back on but was that enough? Was it really worth ending over this? Why had we fought to get this far when we were just going to throw in the towel? It did not feel good. It did not feel right. I could not let this happen.

With that I got up and picked Tom's bike up. Oh dear. The front brake/gear leaver was cracked and hanging loosely down. The front wheel was also bent and caught on the front brakes. How on earth were we meant to fix this? Our basic bike maintenance course before we set out had definitely not given us the skills to deal with this level of catastrophe. I decided to try and force the lever back into place. It was hard however I made it hold, he at least would be able to shift gears if he couldn't brake, but hey I had ridden from the first day with only my front brake. How hard could it be? Next it was time to sort out the wheel. I had no idea what to do. I decided to just loosen the front brakes so that the wheel could turn without catching. There we have it, a ride-able bike. Only one snag; there was no one to ride it. I walked around looking for Tom but could not see him. I decided my best bet was to wait around, figuring he would come back sooner or later. I found some shade by lying underneath a bin and waited, hoping he could come back and everything would turn out okay.

Sure enough about half an hour later he came back. We had both had a chance to think and get our thoughts straight. I decided I needed to be more supportive. I would forget the crash, which was in the past, and instead just focus on the here and now. I showed Tom how I had bodged up his bike and that it was now ride-able. He didn't look too impressed and was still ready to throw in the towel. I managed to persuade him to cycle on to find a bike shop or a shaded area where we might be able to fix it better. He reluctantly agreed to it, although in his mind at that point I think he saw it as a lost cause. Without warning he picked up the 100 remaining biscotti and threw them in the bin. He was angry and tremendously fed up.

Over the next couple of hours we had many successes and failures. No bike shop but we did find shade. We fixed it better so that there was only a slight wobble. I tried my hardest to be supportive; eventually Tom's spirits slightly lifted and he agreed to try and get to Turin. Small steps, I agreed this was a good idea; we were less than 100 kilometres from Turin now anyway. We pushed off with a significant cloud over our heads. I could feel tensions were still quite high. The fact we hadn't managed to find anywhere for lunch only added to this. Tom immediately regretted his rash decision of throwing away all his biscuits. However that may have been a good decision. Our water levels were lowering and we had no way of replenishing them.

We pushed on through the heat of the day. There was nowhere to stop and we had lost time so decided it was the best thing to do. It was slow monotonous cycling. Spirits were low, both of us thinking over what happened and how this could be the end when we reached Turin. They were far from happy thoughts. I guess the struggle of the previous 10 days had finally caught up with us; we were struggling now. I then had a change of heart. If this is the last bit of cycling we are going to do then surely we might as well enjoy it? We should at least try and go out on a high? Things weren't as bad as they could be, the sun was shining, the wind was with us; we were in Italy.

I thought to myself that there was no way we could forget what happened. Therefore coming to the conclusion that we should talk about it, get it out in the open, and then put it behind us. It worked. It turned out as Tom had fallen back his brake lever had become caught in one of my bungee cords on my pannier rack. This had attached us together so unable to escape we came crashing down together. A total accident. We forgave each other for what had happened and turned a corner. This was one of the most pivotal moments of the trip. The whole adventure had been in the balance, and still was; only now we knew that we definitely could deal with any problems. We knew that come the end of our trip we would still be best friends.

Immediately the mood was lifted, we were chatting and joking again. Although we did not know how long each of our bikes would last we knew we would just try and get as far as we could. As long as they were ride-able we would be pedalling them and getting closer to home. Since turning north from the Med it certainly did feel like we were turning home. In our minds the Alps would always be the hardest stretch. They were proving to be, though not just because of the cycling. If we completed the Alps it would then be a quick 1000 kilometre sprint through northern Europe, back to Rotterdam and the ferry home. Despite everything that had happened and the conditions of our bikes, at that moment in time I felt we were going to make it home.

It was a good job spirits had lifted because what followed tested us again. We certainly were being trialled today. We had been looking all afternoon for food and water but as of yet to no avail. In southern France there had been no siesta, we were now more northern so why should they have one here? A definite oversight. We were now out of food and the water in our water bottles was dwindling. We had passed a couple of supermarkets however there was no indication of when –if ever- they would re-open. Disaster! We had no choice but to pedal on regardless. We were famished and growing ever more dehydrated under the burning afternoon sun. We stopped almost every half an hour in shade. Our thinking was this would cool us off, reducing the amount of water we lost from sweating. Our water bottles were now empty. We had nothing. There weren't any houses or people of whom we could ask for help. It was continually feeling like someone was trying to tell us to stop, to give in, to give up. We refused to listen. Who needs water anyway? We pushed into the unknown. Mouths were dry and bodies weak. We had one last push in us. We looked ahead on the GPS and saw that the town of Carmagnola was 20 kilometres away. There were supermarkets there. That was our holy grail. We had to make it. There was no point taking breaks now. We had a goal; the sooner we got there the better. I had forgotten about all my cuts and scrapes, the only thing on my mind was water. Obviously, we did need it.

It was a long hard cycle there, the headwind battering us all the time. As we rolled in to town we almost collapsed outside the Aldi. We had made it. Immediately Tom ran in and purchased some Iced Tea. The cool sugary liquid trickled through our parched mouths and down our dry hoarse throats. It was divine. We had finally been rewarded for the perils that we had to deal with. We took several trips in and out of the supermarket and spent a good couple of hours eating around the side of it. We cooked up some tasty pasta and feasted triumphantly on making it through the day. I also took the opportunity of using the stores toilet, which was an experience I never wish to experience. It reminded me of the toilet scene in Danny Boyles film 'Trainspotting', yes it was that bad. This solidified the fact in my mind that I preferred to 'poo with a view' whilst on tour, it's much more hygienic and exciting. If you can call relieving yourself exciting.

We pedalled just outside of Carmagnola looking for a suitable wild camp. Fortunately we found a great one in a field after just a couple of kilometres. We set up camp in the diminishing light and jumped in. Luckily there were no mosquitoes; unluckily it was still over 30°C, baking hot. We settled in for what was the hottest night on record. Another eventful day to reflect on before thoughts drifted into the lull of sleep.

"You're Only Supposed to Blow the Bloody Doors Off"
Cycling Day 12
Carmagnola to Mont Cenis

What a sweaty night. The temperature never dropped below twenty and needless to say that made it difficult getting to sleep. This did not bother us though. Today we were going to reach Turin. Our major Italian city, we had been looking forward to this for a while, it was one of the major points of the trip. We were buzzing. The trials of the previous day had been sent to the back of our minds, we were smiling and despite 11 hard days, we could not wait to heave our bikes up and get pedalling again.

Finally our mosquito bites were fading, becoming just small blemishes on our now bronzed skin. Our faces were growing more unshaven, albeit not that much as we both could barely grow any facial hair. Salt marks were winding their way down our MS Society bright orange vests. We were now looking and feeling like proper travellers. Cheap thrills gave us immense pleasure and we were now surviving on a simple budget of about 5€ per day. Despite still being in Western Europe we were beginning to feel well travelled and more like hardened adventurers. I think this is because it doesn't matter where you go to have an adventure, only the journey you take. In this sense although we had kept to inhabited regions, where food and water are readily available, we had still faced hard decisions and tough times. It is through these experiences that we have grown into 'adventurers', they have given us opportunities to prove ourselves, opportunities that have tested our friendship and the cause of our journey. What has shone through all this is our need, our hunger, to keep pedalling, to keep on going, to experience more, and to finish our journey no matter what.

It was with this mindset that we got up and loaded our bikes this morning. We were resolute. Our bellies were still full from last nights feast, so we decided we would have a celebratory breakfast once we reached Turin, 20 kilometres away.

We smashed those kilometres, pushing really fast. Taking no breaks, as we knew that once we got to the city we would have a good few hours looking around and 'chilling'. The morning was busy, vast amounts of cars snaking their way into the city; we were in the morning rush hour. The cacophony of horns and engines continued to rise the closer we got to the centre. Like the previous cities we had cycled through so far we had done no research into what to do or see in Turin. This may seem a bit narrow-minded however we found it a much more rewarding and fulfilling experience. We were not bound to only go and see the famous tourist destinations but were free to wander and explore an unknown city. We could get to know it easier, get to know the people and understand more about the culture. All we knew going into it was what little information, if any, we had gathered from 'The Italian Job'.

Hesitantly we arrived in Turin; I say hesitantly because like Nice they too have a tram network, I focused hard on making sure my wheels went nowhere near to the tram tracks. Fortuitously I made it unscathed; I had had enough of crashes. We spied an Intermarché as we pedalled along and decided to stop for a classy breakfast. Fresh, warm pastries and baguettes found their way to our mouths as we sat on the steps next to two bins and no doubt inches away from many rats. We did get an awful amount of crazed stares from passers by. We looked out of place, we didn't care though, we were getting smiles wherever we went. It seemed people were genuinely happy to see us, or we might've just had something on our faces, we will never know. One of these instances was where we met a lady and her daughter who looked a couple of years older than us, bronzed Italian skin and long flowing brown hair down to her waist. They were walking towards us as we sat feasting upon our breakfast. The young girl whispered something in her mother's ear, all the while making eye contact with us.

"She wants a bit of you," I joked to Tom.

At this point both women fix eye contact with us as if they have heard what I said. They then proceed to walk past us and joke about how we are eating off the floor like animals. Yes we had now sunk that low. Everyone looked down on us, even if in a jovial manner. Tom still maintained that he had a chance with her. I now had my doubts. We obviously were beginning to look very bedraggled and like hard faring travellers. Finally! That was the whole point of going on this trip, to get a killer tan, some funny stories, and to look like badass long-distance cyclists. Well according to Tom that was the point. I convinced myself that raising the money for the MS Society was still once of the main focuses. Success on that front was going well too! We were still averaging raising just over a pound a kilometre. This fact did spur us on, especially in the hard times. It gave us more reason to push on. The further we pushed the more good we would be able to do because the more money we would raise. However the further we pushed the better our tans would get also, so all in all it was a win-win situation for the both of us.

We pedalled down cobbled streets, under tramlines, down narrow alleyways. Eventually we stumbled upon the Mole Antonelliana. A *mole* is a building of monumental proportions and the Mole Antonelliana is no exception, it towers above all its surrounds making it one of the major landmarks in the city. It plunges 167 metres into the sky and is no doubt a popular tourist attraction. However we were there early on a weekday morning, so were able to cycle around almost by ourselves. The peacefulness of the tower and dome offered a stark contrast to what was beginning to brew on the roads. We could hear it beginning to get louder as the morning stretched on, soon we would have to cycle out through it. I can say now we weren't looking forward to it that much. We were not going to leave though until we had found a mini. Call us naïve but that was one of our main objectives in Turin that morning. It seemed like a fun idea, searching for a mini, and it would give us an opportunity to see the city. Fear not, we found quite a few. It almost surprised us that we did to be honest; as the Italians are probably not too keen of the Italian Job film.

It was late morning before we decided to leave Turin. We made the decision to try and still have a productive day in the saddle. However my legs were still aching from yesterdays exploits. Fingers crossed there would be no mountains today. I knew there would be, it was inevitable, we were heading to Geneva in the heart of the Alps. I had no chance. Fortunately after we had stocked up on some food and drink to last us the day, and Tom had retrieved his wallet from the supermarket where he had left it *again*.

Huge mountains towered over us on either side. Yet somehow we were doing no climbing. The SS-25 was turning out to be a very pleasant road indeed. We tootled along having a carefree day. It was safe to say the previous few days had taken years off our lives. Finally we thought we were getting used to the mood swings you have whilst long distance cycling, we were much fitter and we were learning how to almost 'switch off' on the bike. All this came together in a subtle serendipity which made the day all that more enjoyable.

We eventually spotted a cluster of trees and decided to take a relaxing hour off for lunch. There were fewer trucks on this road, which non-surprisingly had made us very peaceful. However the sun was getting up and it was getting hot. Another day of beautiful weather, at least some aspects of this trip we were blessed. The laziness had begun. The heat and food had made us tired and we found it nigh impossible to heave our bikes up and mount them again. We had also during lunch looked ahead at the route. Much to our dismay the road turned off the river and began to curve and twist sharply. We knew this meant one thing. Climbing. It looked like we would reach the base of the climb at about 4 and would probably spend the rest of the day climbing. Well we sure would sleep well tonight.

Instead of start the hard work straight away we decided to take a 'well-earned' break at the foot of Mont Cenis. We would need all the energy we had to make it up this climb. My legs felt like jelly and I was apprehensive. We would begin the climb in Italy and finish it in France. Well hopefully we would. Knowing our luck something disastrous would happen during the climb; I wondered what would it be this time?

So it began. We climbed and we climbed, I'll spare you the monotonous detail of the pain we had to go through. We could not see elevation contours on our map only the turns of the road. This was not a good sight. We carried on our 40 minutes on to five minutes off until we could pedal no more. We would have to come up with a new strategy to tackle this mountain; it felt beyond us. We decided to have our short breaks every couple of hundred metres we went up in altitude, this was much nicer. It meant we would be rewarded for going through steep sections and the harder we pushed the quicker we got to have a breather for a couple of minutes. It was a simple idea but effective, and much needed with two heavily laden bikes and shocking gear ratios. It was a long slog and never seemed to end. However it was beautiful. The higher we went the more pretty it got. The great expanse of blue above our heads filled with a few balls of cotton wool. The trees had almost all disappeared, giving us a huge view out down the valley and up towards the snow covered peak of Mont Cenis. Yes snow, it may have been mid July however there was still snow. We kept pushing as it got harder and harder. It felt as if the mountain was trying to pull us back down, it was not letting us go any further up. This actually happened for a three-kilometre section. The Italian government had decided it was a good day to resurface the road, this meant we had a three-kilometre slog at a 10 percent gradient with the asphalt sticking to our wheels not letting us go. As you can imagine that was a *very* fun section to cycle. We stopped afterwards to clean our tyres of the hot sticky tar that covered them. It took a good while for them to stop sticking to the road though.

Eventually we crossed the border into France. Hallelujah! We could now start looking for a place to camp. That was our goal for the day, to finish Italy. It was an odd sensation completing a country, knowing we would never cross back into it again on our journey. Italy especially, a lot had happened over the past couple of days, good and bad. We had become stronger because of our experiences here and had been humbled by the Italians hospitality and good driving. We both knew this would not be the last time we would cycle in Italy in our lives.

Unfortunately although it did flatten out once reaching France we made the mistake of looking up from our handlebars at the road ahead, an almost sheer cliff with the road winding up magnificently. We were now over 1800 metres above sea level and had been climbing for about 15 kilometres. I was broken. My legs had disappeared a couple of kilometres ago and I was struggling. What had I got myself into? I could not face more climbing but I also refused to get off and walk my bike. I was in a catch-22. Luckily I had Tom by my side, he motivated me to pedal and although he was much faster than me we both finally made it to the top. No, we weren't at the top. Once at the top of the cliff we realised the road continued to climb around the Lac du Mont Cenis. Thankfully though the road was at a much more manageable gradient now.

Our water bottles were now empty after that mammoth climb and keen not to repeat yesterday's drought we knocked on the door of a hotel to see if they would fill up our bottles. We were successful, unfortunately rooms were still expensive, there was no 'off-season' for them, we would have to camp. I was thrilled with this reply as I was loving wild camping; and to camp on top of a mountain above a dazzling sapphire blue lake would be a dream.

First though there was the small matter of dinner. We cycled on a short while and came across a bar that seemed to be filled with Russian truck drivers. We elected to sit outside away from everyone and cook up some pasta on our stove. We feasted on what felt like the most deserved meal ever, even more so than yesterday's famine. Today we had certainly earned our food. Unfortunately the bar tender did not think so and refused to let us sit on his chairs unless we bought some drinks. We amused him and obliged, drinking to our successful ascent of the Col du Mont Cenis. No, we were not yet at the top. However we were now over 2000 metres above sea level, above the snow and clouds. We felt hardcore.

After our triumphant meal, we continued to pedal. We would not be disturbed during the night no matter where we camped here but still cycled on to find a place which felt 'right'. We had to go through this rigmarole every night, it is an odd sensation when you finally realise that this is the place that you are going to camp in. Many times it is very similar to previous spots you have found. However I think you develop almost a sixth sense in detecting spots where you will be able to sleep undisturbed. We found a perfect spot, one to rival all those days earlier in the field of sunflowers. This may have just topped it though. We were secluded, looking over the vast tranquil Lac du Mont Cenis, it shimmered in the diminishing light. As we put the tent up we immediately blended into the mountain, hidden from everywhere. We had done it. It had nearly killed us, but we had done it. A fun day of cycling, camping, and sightseeing, topped off with a panoramic camp spot under the stars. Finally we were going to have a nice, cool, nights sleep. It felt well deserved and it was wondrous.

Downhill
Cycling Day 13
Mont Cenis to Argentine

The sunlight burst over the snowy mountain tops and illuminated our tent. That was the best night's sleep of the whole trip. It got nice and cool during the night, which felt like the relief we needed from the stifling day temperatures. We had now camped on top of a mountain. It was peaceful, there were no cars, and all we could hear was the trickling of a nearby mountain stream. We knew we were in paradise, that made it all the more difficult to leave. Despite the majestic night of seamless sleep my legs still felt battered. The past two days had without doubt been the hardest so far. They had been testing and we were now over two kilometres in the air, we had come out on top so far. No doubt we would have another big ascent this afternoon though. I just hoped my legs would have recovered by then.

Again we regrettably had no food for breakfast so had no option but to carry on unfed. We had grown used to this routine by now though so it wasn't much of a hardship. We were just a little bit worried that there wouldn't be anywhere for a while, we still had a little bit more climbing to do and then a descent before there were any signs of a town.

We pushed off, our bikes feeling heavier than ever. Tom had also managed a decent night's sleep despite his sleeping mat failing him as usual. He had laid out his clothes and that combined with the soft ground made for a comfy bed. Finally we made it to the highest point so far 2104 metres above sea level! The air was very thin now and we noticed it. At least it would be downhill now. We were wrong, instead the road just went flat, we cycled around the mountain until our dreams were fulfilled, an open boulangerie. Wahoo! We practically ran inside to buy pain au chocolates and some baguettes. All were just out of the oven and tasted fantastic. We were beside ourselves with our luck. You never know what lies around the corner.

Feeling satisfyingly more plump we mounted our bikes to descend Mont Cenis. I really wanted to savour our elevation so just hoped that the descent would be very gradual and our day would be easy. Initially I was very wrong, we flew down. We zoomed past ski lifts, snow and through the clouds. We also passed some unfortunate cyclists heading the opposite direction, I was very glad I wasn't them. However I do think the side we climbed was harder, that was why it was the longest climb of the Giro d'Italia in 2013.

"That was the best downhill I have done in my life," said Tom.

"Yeah even with just two brakes between us!"

We had plummeted 600 metres in 12 kilometres and it had taken us less than 20 minutes. We had now reached a small plateau in the ski town of Lanslebourg-Mont-Cenis. It was now warming up and turning into yet another sunshine filled day, it was going to be hot. We looked back at where we had come from and were impressed. We had already done 20 kilometres and not even broken a sweat. Fingers crossed this downhill would continue. Luckily it did. Maybe today would be our lucky day? It certainly felt like we were overdue one. We stopped in Termignon at an Intermarché to get some much needed supplies for lunch, and of course a few litres of Iced Tea Lemon. We were truly doing a supermarket tour of Europe.

On a caffeine induced high we continued to descend, it just wouldn't stop. However we weren't complaining. We took the opportunity to have a much needed rest, let our muscles relax and just chill, all the while covering good mileage.

"What would you give Anchorman?" Asked Tom

The conversation had now moved off Lord of the Rings and Top Gear and was verging on something slightly more philosophical, though not quite. We were now scoring films out of 10; I don't know why it just seemed like a good idea. We were stuck though. We both have a profound unconditioned love for Will Ferrell and his appallingly good films. Anchorman, which is without doubt one of the most quotable movies of all time (perhaps second to Airplane), was definitely our favourite. However we eventually could only give it a 6/10, now we do like Ferrell however we came to the conclusion that although comedy was our favourite genre it did not produce our favourite films which we gave the highest ratings to. This pointless realisation turned the mood slightly sombre, till we remembered some more quotes and then were in hysterics until we reached Modane.

We went into the supermarket looking for some snacks, and of course Iced Tea Lemon, however I came out with something quite different. I spied a school notebook for sale and decided to get it and begin writing a diary. I had never written a diary before in my life. However I found it a great way to flesh out the day's events, my thoughts, and thought it would be a good thing to look back on. It was one of the best decisions I made on the trip. I now have something to look back on, without which this book probably would not have been possible. However I was playing catch up, having to write up the 12 previous days as well. I enjoyed this experience and it gave me something to do in my free time. I was reliving the trip whilst still being on it. It was fun. It made me appreciate what we had been through, how we had changed so far and how we had adapted to life on the road. It made me think and reflect on those first few days and how hard they were mentally. The diary served as not only past events but a portal into my memories of life during our cycle. It is this reason why I will take a diary on every future cycle I go on and why I recommend it to people. You don't have to write much, just enough to evoke the memories in your mind.

We stopped for lunch in the town of Saint-Michel-de-Maurienne, eating our food under some trees in a disused campsite. It was baking now! Well over 30°C and we were loving it. Amazingly somehow we were still going downhill! We had done 60 kilometres now and were still 700m above sea level. You may be thinking 60 kilometres doesn't seem like much. Well we had changed our strategy through the Alps, instead of having a rest day we decided we would just push 100 kilometre days through the Alps, this would lighten our load and make the climbs much more manageable, well that was the idea. It was working well so far; we hadn't had to do any climbing. We were basking having some Pasta Bolognaise and only had about 40 kilometres left to cycle, how hard could it be?

It wasn't! The afternoon absolutely sailed by. We continued to wind our way down carving a path down the D1006 through the mountains. We followed the river l'Arc for the rest of the day, this reassured us that we were going downhill. It had definitely flattened out but thankfully was slightly downhill. This helped us battle into the almighty headwind which had risen up. Well we needed something to make this day a bit more difficult!

We took breaks sporadically throughout the afternoon and couldn't help but notice how the weather was changing. Gone was the sun, it had been replaced by ominous clouds; which were growing more threatening by the minute, darker and blacker. We decided we had better stop taking breaks and push to get the last few kilometres done so that we could look for a place to camp and eat.

For the first time in the whole trip I was worried about the rain. We had both grown up in Manchester so had grown very accustomed to rain. However we had now gone two weeks without even a drop. Now we were in the Alps, Europe's largest mountain range, the rain here would be no doubt torrential. Now it wasn't the prospect of rain that bothered us, it was the consequences of it. We had not tested the tent or any of our things in the rain. We did not want to have to get into cold sodden clothes, which is not an experience you want to have to do more than once. Fortunately, we found a great picnic spot beside l'Arc and decided that it would be a perfect place to cook up some dinner. We sat with our toes almost dipped into the river and totally forgot about where we were or the weather. We feasted on some chicken curry and rice; we were also getting a dab hand at this camp-cooking malarkey, if I do say so myself.

We chatted about the days ahead, tentatively suggesting that we were almost on the home stretch. If we made it out of the Alps it would certainly feel like that! Hopefully in a couple of days we would reach Geneva, our next major city and our short-term goal. This helped us a lot having short-term goals of major cities to look forward to. Even if we preferred being in the countryside, going through major cities gave the impression of real movement. Especially in Europe where there are so many you can sometimes hit a few major cities in a day. It gave our cycling added purpose and direction. Giving us something to focus our efforts on, something to push towards. I am glad we planned our trip, in this way because it really made some unbearable days easy, and some easy days great.

During all our daydreaming and eating we had foolishly forgotten about the weather and the seemingly pressing need to find a place to camp. A huge roll of thunder shocked us back to our senses. We packed up like lightning; and sped off wilfully searching for anywhere sheltered we could set up our tent. Just as the first few drops began to fall we found somewhere. Well we thought we did, just as we were getting the poncho out to lie on the ground we noticed a huge ants nest, no thank you. We did not want a repetition similar to our mosquito fiasco.

Regretfully we would have to head out into the shower and leave this otherwise perfect camping spot. It felt as though the rain was about to get much stronger. We were desperate. Then shining like a beacon through the misery was a hydro-power station. Result. There was a large stretch of grass next to it; the station looked very empty, it was ideal for wild camping.

I don't think we have ever moved as fast as we did then. We had the tent up within 2 minutes, our stuff was inside and everything was dry. Just was we were getting inside it stopped. All that rushing for nothing. The storm obviously was in a neighbouring valley and well out of sight. Instead of getting out to look around a bit more we decided to just read our books and get an early night instead. We had cycled downhill for over 100 kilometres! Albeit mostly into a headwind but 100 kilometres downhill is a dream. We knew this would be short-lived and we would no doubt have to begin climbing in the morning. However we felt that the brutal climb up Mont Cenis was certainly worth it. I had a slight suspicion that tonight's sleep was not going to be as good as yesterdays. However I told myself to stop over thinking everything as usual and to just get a good nights rest for tomorrow's inevitable climb.

SLUGS!
Cycling Day 14
Argentine to Beaumont

My suspicions of a bad nights sleep were wrong, I woke up and my legs were feeling good and I was refreshed. The mountain air was doing us good, also the air felt a lot thicker at this altitude. Unfortunately upon waking I realised we had a problem. Our hurry to find a good camping spot had turned out to be a bit of a rash decision. We had been infiltrated. Slime oozed everywhere; they were sliding over the tent in all directions. Their trails formed intricate patterns across the tent membrane. Slugs! Slugs! Slugs! Slugs! Massive oozing SLUGS! We were beginning to feel like all wildlife was inexplicably attracted to us. First we were eaten alive by mosquitoes and now we had been infested by slugs. These were no normal slugs either; these were huge, bulbous, oozing, orange, mutants. They were disgusting. Somehow we made it out of the tent unscathed, it was now time to face them and pack up. They were everywhere. You name the place they were there. We flicked, shook, prodded, and threw them in all directions. I know this may seem a little harsh but try and imagine all your worldly possessions covered in slugs, we wanted them off. It was a lengthy process, how on earth had they got everywhere? I though slugs were meant to be slow moving. Not these ones, these were the Usain Bolt's of the slug world, they darted about everywhere, constantly trying to get back onto and into our things.

It was the longest start to the day of the whole trip. It took us over an hour and a half to clear everything of slugs, yes there were that many, and getting rid of the majority of the slime was a task in itself.

We were a bit worried at one point when a man showed up in his car and went into the power station. However when he came out he was all smiles and wished us good luck on our journey. It is these moments that stick out the clearest in my mind. Random acts of kindness and generosity. This man could've quite easily told us to move and get off the land however he empathised with us and showed true kind human nature. This is the greatest thing about cycle-touring, meeting people who help you and are genuinely lovely human beings. It reaffirms your self-belief, makes you lighten up and makes you think about how you act around complete strangers. Why not just give people a smile? It may just brighten up their day.

He had this effect on us. Our initial hatred for the morning, more precisely the slugs, was calmed. We smiled and began to once again realise the hilarity of the situation we were in. What on earth were we doing? We did not know. We had spent long enough messing around and thought it was high time we start pedalling away. So we began, our 14th consecutive day of cycling around Europe, we had had no breaks and we were going stronger than ever!

Although the rain had been short-lived last night, today was far from bright and sunny. It was a grey overcast day. This in a weird way was comforting to us, it reminded us of Manchester, this was the weather we were used to cycling in. Today, despite its appalling start, was going to be a good day. We stopped in the town of Aiguebelle for breakfast. Our usual Pains au Chocolates with Baguettes, unfortunately we had to settle for Peach Iced Tea –it just wasn't the same.

We continued until we had cycled the entire length of the D1006, it was a tearful moment when we finally had to leave it. Then we joined the incredibly flat D1090, which would take us to Frontenex where the days climbing would begin. It was a calm morning; the previous day had acted like a recover day because of the lack of climbing. We now felt like seasoned pros capable of completing any Tour de France stage.

Although it was not raining it was the greyest day of our cycle so far. Clouds shrouded the peaks around us; we were encased on all sides by the fearsome undulations that we would no doubt soon have to climb. We left the valley at Frontenex and turned directly up the Col de Tamié. It was tough, short, and steep. We took a quick pause halfway to re-lube up our chains, suddenly our feet could spin easier and the climbing was eased. However that only lasted for a few brief moments, before we knew it the lactic acid was once again building up in our quads. I was out of my seat pumping my legs, trying to use my body weight to gain some inertia to push me up the mountain. We saw no other cyclists on this climb; it probably wasn't the weather for it. Instead we rode up in solitude with no cars passing us also. Despite the grey surrounds it was a lovely mountain pass. Rich green trees sprang from every rock giving the hillside a lush appearance. The moisture rich air soothed our faces as we climbed higher and higher. We had gone back to taking breaks every 200 metres in altitude, this worked better for us when we were ascending. Finally the GPS altimeter clicked over to 907 metres above sea level and we completed the climb. Wahoo! It had been a tough 11 kilometres; however we were hoping to be rewarded by a lovely long descent now.

We were. Not as long as yesterdays however it was sublime, we drifted down past farms and pastures for 20 kilometres. Eventually we made it to Faverges and decided to stop and have some lunch. Unfortunately it isn't the biggest town so we had to make do with a very small supermarket. We managed to come out with some tinned ravioli, not the healthiest meal however it did say it contained 100% beef, although on reflection it was most probably horse meat. Despite no doubt being filled with saturates they were pretty tasty, we both had opted for 500 gram (huge size) tins so by the time we had finished we were nicely full. They had certainly filled a hole, washed down with some lemon iced tea, it was a perfect meal. The wind was picking up though and boy was it chilly. We still had our fingers crossed for a sunny afternoon though because despite the wind it was beginning to look a lot brighter.

We would head around Lake Annecy this afternoon and try and get as close to the Swiss border as we could, that was the plan. Fortunately the wind was, for once, behind us. We were able to sail past families on their cycling holidays' and zoom around the huge lake. The French government had done well for this stretch because we were able to use a cycle path that stretched for 14 kilometres around the coast of the lake. Yes, this is a big lake. It is the second largest in France and also weirdly known as "Europe's Cleanest Lake", Tom and I refrained from swimming though. It wasn't the day for swimming in icy glacial water.

The further we went round the brighter it got. Hotter and hotter we became until we were back to wearing our usual attire of our bright orange MS Society running vests. Although not designed for cycling they were great, they offered superb breathability, unmatchable visibility, and most importantly for Tom they meant we would get a more even tan. We were both enjoying updates of how our fundraising was going on back in the UK. My mum was logging on to our Just Giving internet page every day giving a little update on how we were getting on. I think it worked well, people could see how their money was propelling us around Europe and how it was going to make a difference to so many peoples lives. It really did propel us, every time we heard a new update of how much we had raised we became lifted. It gave us a sense, a purpose, to cycle and to keep cycling. We could feel good about ourselves and about the people we were benefiting at the same time. It hadn't taken much effort to set up the donation page and send out a few emails and tweets. The re-tweet from Ewan McGregor certainly did help us gain awareness. It was all easy, much easier than the cycling, and that is why I think everyone should do sponsored events and sponsor events of friends and family. It doesn't take much to donate just a little, but what you do donate will be generously received and heartfelt.

Suddenly we rounded a corner on the baking afternoon and saw an idyllic rest stop. The road sunk down to a small stream that was flowing out of the wood, picnic tables were sporadically dotted around the light stone path. The whole area was sparkling in the afternoon sunlight. It looked magical. We only had 10 kilometres left to cycle till we would camp so we decided to take a well earned rest and relax for a couple of hours. It was sublime, one of the best siestas we had taken the entire trip. We managed to stretch out the tent in the sunlight so it dried out, we read our books, listened to some music, and wrote messages home. This break was what we had needed; we began to appreciate once again where we were and what we were doing. One thing Tom appreciated a lot was the wooden cabin, which turned out to be a toilet with a seat! Ah such luxury. We stayed a long while, till our shadows grew tall. We then decided it would be a good idea to cook up some pasta and have some dinner. We would then cycle on for 30 minutes and look for somewhere to camp. It was peaceful, although right off the D1021, we felt secluded. We were in our own little world. Fortunately there were no mosquitoes or slugs. However at one point I took off my shoe to let my feet breathe a little. To my own horror the entire end of my sock was dyed yellow, I immediately thought a huge blister had popped and oozed out inside my shoe. However once I inspected my shoe a dead and very squashed slug dropped out of it, lovely, 85 kilometres of cycling with a slug in my shoe.

Sadly eventually the sun was threatening to dip below the mountains and it was time we had to leave our wonderland. It had been by far the best afternoon stop we had made, the best way to relax. We pedalled on sedately stopping at a supermarket to get some food for breakfast and lunch, tomorrow would be a Sunday and we knew all to well what that meant in Europe, nothing would be open. Eventually we came across an odd sight, so odd it merited us stopping and going to investigate what it was. The road separated as it passed over the river 'Les Usses' as we crossed over the steep tree lined valley we saw a magnificent bridge, the Pont de la Caille. Yes we may be a little bit sad, but this bridge looked awesome. It looked new yet was in a medieval design, transporting us back to the time of the crusades. We cycled over to go have a look at it, it was huge and magnificent offering a 360 degree panoramic view back to Lake Annecy and on towards Geneva and Switzerland. There were two huge white stone towers at either side of the valley from which the bridge was suspended, like a more rustic golden gate bridge. We just couldn't fathom why it was there though. Although it was spectacular it was weird and very out of place amongst the natural setting of the valley.

On and on we cycled till we were less than 5 kilometres from the Swiss border, the D1021 had turned out to be quite busy so we were struggling to find any good camping spots at the side of the road. We were relaxed though we had been in this situation many times before now and we had always found somewhere. Sure enough eventually we found a great spot in a farmer's field. We were right next to the road but out of sight thanks to some bushes. Upon putting up the tent we became invisible, it blended seamlessly with the grass of the field. All we could do was hope this would be a slug-less night.

The Final Climb
Cycling Day 15
Beaumont to Champagnole

We rose bright eyed and bushy tailed, it had been a great night's sleep. We didn't wake once, it was not too hot, and the nearby D1201 kept nicely quiet. It was a mere 7am and being a Sunday, France was still asleep. We were both smiling because in an hour or two we would be cycling through country number five and the city of Geneva.

This is one of the great things about Europe you can wake up and have breakfast in one country, have lunch in another and be onto your third by dinner time. You can sample a lot of culture and people in a short space of time, and distance. We had a few packets of crêpes whilst we took down the tent —these had become our new favourite food, great to eat on the bike or if you just are feeling peckish in the morning. On good days we would easily go through two packets of 12 each. It's all about getting the calories in when you are cycling long distances, as we were burning over 7000 calories each every day.

Carrying all our litter with us, making sure we left nothing behind; we loaded the bikes and set off to cover the last 20 kilometres into Geneva. It was a blast. It certainly all felt like it was downhill, even though it probably wasn't. We were just filled with adrenaline and anticipation. Once we cleared Geneva we would almost be out of the Alps and then we could begin our final assault on the UK. 'Once the Alps are out of the way it's just a short smash across northern Europe to get the ferry home,' that was our mentality. We had broken it up into chunks and hopefully today, all going well; we would discard one of those chunks and that would allow us to begin the final push. Although that final push was 1000 kilometres, we saw that as only a minor detail.

It was another grey beginning to the day; though we had faith that it would brighten up later on, as it always had. Ten minutes of rain in 15 days wasn't too bad, especially for two boys from Manchester, we intended to keep up our record of good weather so put our sunglasses on in the hope that optimism would bring the sun out. The grey clouds seemed to be holding in all the moisture making it very humid, so needless to say it wasn't long before we were drenched in sweat. I can't even remember now the last time we had a shower, it was probably in Nice. Every day our tans would thicken, our beards would grow (only kidding we couldn't grow facial hair), and our once shiny orange Multiple Sclerosis vests would gain an extra layer of sweat and dirt. They were now looking more brown than orange. We had lost the point in caring in our appearance. There was little point in making an effort. There was no one to impress but each other. If we did want to spend time and effort cleaning our clothes then they would simply become dirty within a couple of hours, we just saw no point in it. Call us disgusting but we were lazy and really had bigger things to focus on. Or maybe we just had a total disregard for personal hygiene and had grown to enjoy being dirty.

It was a cool morning, the air felt sharp in our lungs and dew threatened to stick to our hair. Speaking of hair, our once silky smooth legs were gradually becoming more masculine again, albeit only a few hairs poking up. We were rugged explorers and had travelled through many lands, in our heads, to reach this point; it was now time to enter Switzerland.

It's amazing the difference a border makes. You cycle just a few metres and BOOM you are in a whole different culture, a whole different currency and a whole different way of life. We cycled through the desolate border point, no one was in sight but it still felt different. Our bikes make a different sound on the smooth asphalt, the houses were different and everything was clean. We knew we must be in Switzerland. Like all the other cities we had visited we had no plan of what to do once we got to Geneva. We just pedalled around sedately and experienced the atmosphere. That was what we found odd; it was hard to find anything. Nothing was open and no one was around, anywhere. We knew Sundays are pretty much no-go days in Europe but we assumed that Geneva being a major city would have a bit more hustle and bustle at almost 10am.

Eventually we were roused by the sound of a megaphone and what else could we do but go check it out? It was coming from right down on the Lake, which looked pretty windy today; we were hoping for a tailwind later. It turned out that there was a big triathlon going on. It looked pretty professional so Tom and I spent a good while wheeling our bikes around and marvelling at all the amazing bikes on show. There was so much carbon. Okay, moment over. We were happy though for another reason, for once we were not the most lycra-clad people around. We looked normal compared to these skin-suits, well if normal meant covered in dirt and stinking, which I am pretty sure it doesn't. However you get my gist. We eventually discovered that it was the International Triathlon of Geneva, it all sounded very impressive. Truth be told we were a little envious of these guys. They were all getting their massages, energy drinks, and extra superfluous treatment. What did we have? A couple of bottles of iced tea, heavy and laden bikes oh and sun-cream, but there was no way that I was going to give Tom a massage with it. Despite all this we liked to jest that we could give them a run for their money, we had been training for it for the past 15 days of course.

It was a lovely relaxed morning in Geneva; we even got to use a flushing toilet! Think of the novelty. It was just a shame all of the shops were shut and there wasn't many people about. I really wanted to get a Swiss army knife, and then I would be a true explorer. Unfortunately every single shop was shut so we had no option but to...yes you guessed it, keep on pedalling. Wahoo!

I say that like it was becoming a bore but it really wasn't. We were loving it more than ever, now we had found ways to deal with the daily stresses, the cycling, the sleeping and they were all just second nature now. We had totally adapted to life on the road. Even our bodies were changing shape and becoming more adjusted to life in the saddle, our legs getting bigger and our arms losing all bulk and just gaining definition, luckily we didn't have much bulk to lose in the first place. Somehow by just pedalling in a North Westerly direction we found our way back to the route and out of Switzerland. We plummeted underneath the runway of Geneva International Airport and out onto the D1005, we were back into France. Boy was France pleased to see us, like that the sun came out, the clouds went away and it was baking once again.

This was going to be a good day, despite thinking this we knew it would be hard. When we were planning the route we knew that the climb out of Geneva was massive however hopefully that would be our last big climb of the Alps. Hopefully... We were now at just 400 metres above sea level and climbing at a steady gradient. No doubt soon we would start up a Col though and it really would get tough. It did. It was fun though, the good weather had brought out lots of other cyclists, from tourers to semi-pro's and they all seemed to be cycling the Col de la Faucille. It did not compare to Mont Cenis though, or perhaps Mont Cenis made us stronger? Anyway we made it to the top in one piece, praying for a lovely long descent out of the Alps.

We feasted at the top, 1319 metres above sea level, on some chicken cous cous, so good they named it twice we joked. We were rewarded with fantastic views back over Lake Geneva, the water now glistening in the sunlight. It was peaceful.

After lunch we put our jackets on for what would no doubt be a fast and chilly descent. We zoomed through the trees at 60kph, touching the apexes at the corners, and flying down the mountainside. The climb was definitely worth it now, fingers crossed it would last to the end of the day. We almost were able to free-wheel all the way to the town of Morez. When we got there we were carving our way down the valley when in front of us lay a mountain. We saw a road carving its way up and around it. Almost simultaneously we both gulped. I looked down at the GPS; yep we would be cycling on that road. The climbing was not over for the day. Initially it was steep and out of the saddle hard work, it then turned into a long uphill slog until eventually we summited again at 991 metres above sea level, this time on the Col de la Savine. If we weren't tired before we certainly were now. We were dead, two big climbs and not nearly enough Iced Tea. If only we could get some more, but it was a Sunday so we could only hope. Fortunately after the summit we could relax and freewheel down the hillside. The sun was getting lower in the sky and suddenly it seemed like the whole day had just disappeared. It had gone so fast. We were in definite need of a rest stop so when a picnic area opened up next to the road we did the natural thing. Jumped off our bikes, lay on the ground and relaxed.

"Ahhhhhhh, at last," We sighed.

We lay there for a good hour until we felt suitably recovered then we decided we would pedal on another 10 kilometres or so and eat, then go on and find a place to camp. We had taken to this idea of eating in a separate place to where we were camping; it seemed to work for us in different ways. It meant we were spending the minimum amount of time in the place where we were staying so we were less likely to get caught. We were eating in a different place so hopefully flies, ants etc. would not be attracted to our sleeping area. We were well fed when we were looking for a place to camp, this meant that tensions were not running high, there was no pressure to find anywhere quickly and we avoided stress. All in all this method worked.

We were sprawled out on the tarp, just boiling the first batch of water to cook the pasta, the sun was going down and we were basking triumphantly (as we normally did) on the days cycling. This was when all of a sudden a car pulled up. We both thought it looked a bit dodgy. Until, yet again, we were shown a great act of kindness from another human being. A man proceeded to get of his car and run over to us. We were not sure what was happening. When suddenly he revealed what he was hiding in his hands, four lovely ripe apricots. He handed them to us, wished us a good day and good luck on our travels and then he was gone as quick as he had arrived. We were in awe, I know it may only seem like just a few apricots but this man had gone to the trouble of turning around, pulling over and giving them to us. We were two very grateful boys and were suddenly uplifted. If only everyone was this generous and friendly, the world would be an even nicer place to live in. It made me think about my own life as well, would I have pulled over to two dirty cyclists and given them some fruit? Honestly, I probably wouldn't have. It has been drilled into me from a young age to be cautious of strangers, my nana would warn, "Don't get in peoples cars they could be paedophiles" etc. but in fact people are awesome. Strangers can help you; they can become good friends. All throughout our trip we had seen instances of how kind people can be. Would we get the same treatment back in the UK? I liked to think we would but I wasn't too sure. Just this small act of this man giving us some apricots has changed my outlook. Now I would stop to give those travellers something, even if it was just a good luck. Something that small can uplift your spirits; just share the love a bit. This hit me in a crystallising moment when I took a bite into that deliciously juicy apricot. I remembered the faces of all the people that had helped us and I will never forget them. Without these strangers we would have failed, lost our drive and lost all hope. It is with thanks to them that we had made it this far. We had conquered the Alps!

We ate our meal, our faith in humanity restored. We were also doubly happy because we found out that Mark Cavendish had won the Champs-Élysées for his fourth consecutive year making him the most successful sprinter in tour history with 23 stage wins. We also heard the if not bigger news that Bradley Wiggins had won the Tour de France being the first ever Briton to do so. We proudly rode on until sunset and just outside the town of Champagnole. We were on the N5 which was quite major so it took a while to find a good place to camp. Eventually we got the tent up though and settled in, buzzing with excitement. No more mountains! Tomorrow we would try and clear the foothills and finally say 'adieu aux Alpes'.

We Really are Finally Getting Somewhere
Cycling Day 16
Champagnole to Gray

We slept like champions. We felt as if we had completed a feat akin to reaching the North Pole. We had finished the Alps. In reality we had just cycled over a few mountains for a few hundred kilometres. I say 'just', in reality it was hard and the hardest cycling we had ever done in our lives. However we had built it up so much in our minds we imagined them uncrossable and our goal nigh unattainable. In fact the mental strength we had gained over the previous fortnight had prepared us for the trials and tribulations we would have to face. It was a different type of cycling though. So far on our trip on most of the days we would be battling with our minds, our bodies could keep on going monotonously however it was our thoughts that threatened to upturn our pursuit of victory. In the mountains this was a different story, we found our minds occupied, albeit mostly with pain, however this focus gave us a new mental drive. Mentally the mountains were easier; we would have one big climb then a lovely long easy descent. Physically they were hard although not impossible. We found our rhythm and then turned the pedals a few thousand times.

We were now out. Back onto the glorious roads of the French countryside. They really were wonderful, the asphalt lovely and smooth, nothing on Switzerland but still miles better than anything we had cycled on in the UK. If the French manage without pot-holes why can't we? They have a much larger road network than us and a similar sized population, so it can't be lack of man-power.

We were loving it; the thought of not having to climb another mountain was one we warmly greeted. Another great feeling was starting the day with a downhill. Today was going to be a good day; we were ahead of our target pace for the trip so could afford to take a couple of rest days. Instead we liked the idea of just doing shorter mileage for many days. We liked doing about 120 kilometres and found it was a good distance. Not too far, so wasn't too tiring for the legs, day after day. It also was under 6 hours riding at our pace so gave us a nicer relaxed day, for looking around places, taking breaks, and meeting people. Although no doubt the people we did meet probably thought we looked like hobos. Cue discussion about how dirty and ragged we looked. To be honest we liked it; well we liked the tan. I would have preferred it if Tom would use the deodorant that he brought along with him. We were now on day 16 and he was yet to use it. His argument was that he didn't want to get cancer. I let it go though after a while, I was using deodorant and in spite of it I suspect I only smelt marginally better than Tom.

It was shaping up to be yet another glorious day in Western Europe. The sun was shining, the temperature was creeping up towards the thirties, and there wasn't a single cloud in the sky. I mean literally none. We were cycling along a long, straight, flat, poplar tree lined row, we could see the whole expanse of the sky and there was not one single cloud.

What we did see was a small German supermarket, Aldi. As per our usual we pulled in to see what tasty and cheap delights they had on offer. It was mid-morning and we still hadn't had a proper breakfast. Need I say it; we went a bit over board with the food buying. We could have fed Africa with the amount we bought. However hating wastage we made it our task to eat it all, every yogurt, every crepe, every pain au chocolate, every bar of Tom's new favourite European chocolate 'Crunch Bars', every banana, every brioche, I am surprised that the Aldi had enough stock left to keep trading.

An hour later and our jaws were still masticating; the pile of food was now growing a lot thinner. We had conquered the worst of it. We were sat on the ground outside the Aldi and were treated by the biggest expanse of blue sky we had ever seen. There was not a single cloud in visible sight.

This prompted Tom to say to the camera, "We're having such a tough time out here, mosquito's, slugs, mountains, it's been absolutely rotten. Now it seems the weather is turning against us, we've been pedalling for days and not glimpsed the sun once, now it's really hard to keep on pedalling, it's clouding over quite badly."

At this I panned the camera over the vast expanse of blue sky. I am surprised he managed to keep such a straight face, I couldn't stop laughing. Sixteen days and we still were not bored of each others company, phew. As the day was heating up, we became increasingly wary that we had not covered much distance and it was nearing 11. We decided to pack up shop and move our heavily bloated bodies on to the next stop, lunch.

We cycled, we sweated, and we got tired. That was the story for many of our days in the saddle. Today though it was very fitting, the temperature was in the mid-thirties by 12, it was like being back on the Med again. However now we could sweat without getting drops of sun cream in our eyes. Our skin had become accustomed to spending all day in the sun; we were bronzed. We also had a lovely layer of dirt that probably did the job of sun cream for us.

We were now out of the Alps so our daily targets were going to increase from about 110 kilometres, as they had been in the mountains. Today we were aiming for 130 kilometres, a reasonable distance we thought ourselves more than capable after 16 days of training for it. That's in a way how we saw the cycling, every day we would get fitter and in our minds that would prepare us more for the next day. We are not cyclists and didn't do much training before hand. Indeed I don't think you have to train for an adventure like ours. I believe anyone could do what we did, purely because we did it and we are not cyclists. I am not saying it is easy, it is one of the hardest things either of us had done but if you have determination you will succeed, it is that simple. You may not be fit to begin with so start off doing small mileage days, and just keep on lengthening them out, as and when you feel ready.

However Tom and I may have been a little short-sighted when we decided to pedal for 130 kilometres today. We hadn't taken into account one thing, hills. Boy was that an oversight. We were clearly in the foot hills of some sort. Constantly rolling up and down, up and down, up and down. It was hard going in the heat of the day, sapping all the energy from our legs. It is conditions like this when tempers run short and as a team you have to tread carefully as to not upset the balance of each other. I am talking mentally but also physically, you don't want to upset the balance of their bike.

We stopped for lunch at one, we had to, and there was no way we could push on further. We had covered a pitiful 70 kilometres. Barely half our distance we wanted to cover. So much for having a nice downhill coast out of the Alps. This day was pushing us beyond our limits. The weather was lovely, the sun was out, but it felt as though we had lost our rhythm. We were beaten. We walked over to the stone picnic benches at the side of the road and collapsed onto them. Sprawling out and letting our bodies relax. If only we could stay here for longer. We knew we would have to eat a fast lunch and get back on the bikes as fast as possible. This is because for some reason we are always slightly slower in the afternoon, maybe we are tired? However we wanted to make the town of Gray in decent time so that we could stock up on some food for dinner, eat, and then look for a place to camp. Who knows how long that will take? We had a goal and we had a time limit. All we could do was just push out the miles. No matter how hard it was we would just have to push. Better push now and have relaxed final days than relax now and risk missing the ferry back to England. We were now having to think about things like this, we had less than 1000 kilometres to go, it was getting closer but we also still had to remind ourselves that we had two more countries to cross yet, Rotterdam was further away than we thought.

Tom ate his favourite French tinned ravioli, and I ate my favourite chicken cous cous, in record time. Before we knew it we were re-fuelled and ready to go. We were going to smash the afternoon. To cut a long story short, we did. It was some of the hardest cycling of my life, which was weird because we didn't do any massive climbs. There was just an absolutely obscene amount of hills. Up and down we went, though it mostly felt like up. Finally after slogging it for 125 kilometres, through the beautiful French countryside we made it to the town of Gray. Despite its name it is quite a vibrant town and wasn't that boring! We were expecting something like the Valley of Ashes from The Great Gatsby so were rather shocked when we cycled over La Saone, on a bridge covered with flowers, looking over the calm waters and gardens. It was picturesque.

We were so uplifted having made it to our target. We were even more overjoyed when we saw the majestic signs to an Intermarche; we opted against the McDonalds as we were now 'athletes'. Stocking up on some pasta, pesto, and basil, tonight we were going to experiment with the culinary possibilities of our tiny camping stove. We rode out of the town of Gray feeling surprised, as it was not at all how we had envisaged it. Instead it was in keeping with the rest of the towns and villages we had ridden through today, beautifully French.

Just outside the town we pulled over to cook up what hopefully would be the best meal of the trip so far. Well best meal we had prepared, those pizzas in Nice were amazing, as were the kebabs on the first day. We stopped on a nice patch of grass beside the road, it was right next to a war memorial of a soldier who had died during world war one. Tom went about preparing stuff for the meal and boiling the water whilst I spread out the tent and tarps to dry, they had quite a bit of condensation from the previous nights sleep. Then it was time to get down to business. We cooked the little spinach and cheese filled parcels of pasta to perfection, if I do say so myself. We then added some of the tomato pesto and then spread some pre-grated French cheese on top. That was the icing on the cake, absolute perfection. It was by far the tastiest meal we had cooked, the nearby ants and flies also agreed. It felt like a well-deserved treat for the headwind and rolling hills we had battled against all day.

We ate and we ate until our food stocks were running dangerously low. At this point the light was fading and we felt it was high time to pack up our little picnic and head on to find a nice camping spot. We pedalled on for quite a way, as there wasn't anywhere decent for a long while. Eventually while pedalling down the D67, just outside Oyrieres, we spotted a dirt track leading into a wood on the other side of the road. We went down and decided that it looked pretty perfect, the fact that it was in the shade a real bonus because although the light was fading it would have definitely made the tent stifling. We got the tent up in easily under two minutes, feeling like we had mastered the life skill of being able to easily put up a tent we jumped in.

It had been such a hard day, when I looked at the GPS we had climbed over 2,000 metres in total ascent over the day! That was more than an average day in the Alps. No wonder we were tired as most of that was into a horrible wind. It was over now though; hopefully tomorrow will be much more pleasant, we thought to ourselves as we drifted off into another superb nights sleep. I say superb, it was as good as it got when you are sharing a tiny tent with a teenage boy, who hasn't showered for a week, on a mattress just a couple of centimetres thick.

SLUGS! (again)
Cycling Day 17
Gray to Vecqueville

It was a good night's sleep. Long gone are the days of tossing and turning, being awoken by Tom's snoring, we are veteran campers now. We are used to roughing it and have perfected the art of getting a good night's sleep on a thin camping mat. We needed a good night's rest after yesterday as well, two kilometres of ascent; our only hope was that it would flatten out today. Fingers crossed.

When we did awake, we were treated with a horror that felt all too familiar. Slugs! Yet again it felt as if God had sent a plague upon us. Somebody somewhere must have been laughing at all the misfortune that had come our way. However although this time there were quite a few slugs, there were significantly less than a couple of days ago. These slugs did look significantly nastier though. They were long, bulbous, bright orange, slimy things that covered the floor of the wood and our tent. I was careful to check my shoes this time before putting them on. I did not want a soggy sock from a squished slug again. Especially slugs that looked as nasty as these ones. We went about doing what we did best, flicking slugs with sticks, until eventually all the slugs were off our possessions. Then we began the process of taking the tent down, shaking it a few extra times to make sure there were no slugs before putting it in its' stuff sack. Not only were we now amazing at putting the tent up we were a pretty dab hand at getting it down as well. If ever you are in trouble and need an MSR Hubba Hubba assembling, we are your guys.

I felt ready to start cycling however had a niggling at the back of my mind that although I thought I felt fresh my legs were very very very tired. Tom had the same look on his face. We were pretty beaten. It had been days without a bed, days without a wash, and all the while pushing pretty big miles with fully laden bikes. It was beginning to hit us how mammoth our journey was. Although the end was almost in sight, we certainly weren't there yet. We envied the riders of the Tour de France, they didn't have to take their kit on their bikes, they didn't have to cook, they didn't have to camp, they received lovely massages, and they were doing about the same distance as us. Albeit they were cycling at much faster speeds, however that's by-the-by. Tom and I agreed we needed to either become professional cyclists or maybe just go on more normal holidays in the future.

Slowly and painfully we pushed our legs on the pedals and rolled off into the day of cycling. I wanted to say 'sped off' but we were hardly speeding, we were averaging about 22kph. We headed towards the little town of Champlitte where we hoped to find a boulangerie or supermarket of some kind. We were both in need of our Pains au Chocolate and Lemon Iced Tea fix. Fortunately after a lot of searching and receiving different directions from locals we found a supermarket. More importantly they had both of our desires in plentiful stock. We could not have been happier; I think the woman on the till noticed this, our overwhelming joy at something as simple as food and drink. We feasted in the car park for quite a while. Our once early 8am start had drifted away and by the time we got going again we were slightly behind schedule. Although we didn't really have a schedule we just cycled, ate, slept, cycled some more. I was always keen to get as much mileage done in the morning as possible. The roads were quieter and the temperature cooler. However on this particular morning the cycling was tough. Not because of the hills but because we both felt as if we were going to throw up. We had both just drank, pretty much in one, a litre of vanilla drinking yogurt. Extremely tasty however I must say do not try this at home. To say bloated would be an understatement. We were ill.

It was a very slow few kilometres out of Champlitte, which in itself was a lovely little town. A very grand stately home-esque manor in the centre, friendly locals and a well stocked supermarket. Well it was well stocked before we arrived. Out of the town the roads continued to undulate. Yes, more and more hills. I am sure you can tell that we were overjoyed by this. Our minds conjured up dreams of how amazing it would be once we got to the Netherlands. That was quite a way off though. We were about half way from Switzerland to Belgium. Hopefully we would reach it the day after tomorrow; at least that was our plan.

We were enjoying cycling the D-roads of France; they offered a unique tranquillity away from large towns and many cars. It was lovely, just pedalling through the French countryside, through pastures, with the sun beating down upon our backs. We were loving it, even the hills were struggling to get us down, and I know I go on about them a lot. The head wind that we had battled yesterday had disappeared. We were free to pedal on home to England, without a care in the world.

The sun continued to shine and we continued to cycle. That was pretty much the story for the morning. Oh and the road continued to undulate, but you could have probably guessed that. Nothing major happened but our legs grew ever more weary. By the time lunch came around we had already done 1000 metres of ascent. That's similar to a major climb in the Alps!

We stopped for lunch at a roadside picnic stop, which was lovely, slug and mosquito free we really had hit the jackpot. Tom had more of his tinned ravioli favourite and I had my chicken cous cous, both of us washed down our meal with some of Lipton's finest lemon Iced Tea. We also took this opportunity to look ahead at the route. We were wary that although the road had become a lot flatter in the previous couple of kilometres before lunch, it had also become much more major. It was then when our hearts sunk as we realised we would have to navigate the more major road for the rest of the day. Although it was probably more likely to be flatter, it was also more likely to be much busier being an N-road. We would choose hills over traffic any day. French traffic is not like English traffic either, as the majority of vehicles on our roads at home are probably family cars, white vans and the occasional HGV. In France it is the complete opposite, you can tell it is a more industrial country, as huge trucks hurtle down the roads constantly, occasionally followed by a small French hatchback beeping away. The beeps are a continuous cacophony of noise, and are used to mean almost everything. There is the 'get the hell of the road I am going to hit you' beep, the 'Wahoo, a fellow cyclist I wish you well on your journey' beep and literally everything in between. It takes an awful while to get used to this different horn culture and I think Tom and I spent quite a lot of the first two weeks having the life shocked out of us by another car or truck coming up behind us. However now we have become numb to the effects of the horn, thank god, and can cycle on un-phased by the incessant annoyance. One word while I am on the topic of French drivers is that they do have a lot more time for cyclists, perhaps it is because the majority of the roads are less busy, but we have certainly found drivers to almost always give us a good amount of space.

Whilst packing the bikes up after lunch we noticed that Tom's pannier rack was broken. I have lost count of the amount of times something has gone wrong on this trip now. Fortunately, we had experienced his rack breaking before when on our cycle to Paris a year earlier. Tom was cycling onto the ferry at Dover and got hit by a strong crosswind almost sending him down into the water. Luckily he came down inches away from the edge but with his wheel bent and his pannier rack broken. With this in mind I had a good idea of how to fix it. I got out the para-cord from my pannier and began lashing his pannier to his bike. It seemed to work well, we melted it in place using a lighter and then it was a good as new, well not really but it was fixed.

We were on the road again to finish of the rest of today's 130 kilometres. The sun was still shining; we were still dirty, everything was normal. Fortunately the road did flatten out a lot so we were able to push some good fast miles North, creeping ever closer towards Belgium. We just pedalled and chatted the day away; this was what we envisaged the 'holiday' being like. A nice gentle pedal around Europe, having some banter and getting a nice tan. That was what today was like, relaxing. However we were in dire need of a relaxing day, our plan of not taking rest days and just pedalling on regardless was beginning to catch up with us. We were growing weary; the prolonged tiredness was beginning to creep in and we were finding it a real battle to keep going. The strain and stress of what was approaching 3 weeks away was beginning to take its toll. We craved a bed; I think rather then being able to have a good night's sleep we had just become accustomed to having a bad night's sleep. All this built on top of one another and felt like an immense weight, we were tired.

We were also loving Europe though and being away, so despite being absolutely knackered we pedalled on, taking in the amazing French countryside around us. As ever we were looking forward to dinner. Last night had been such a triumph on the food front, tonight we would try and match it with tortellini in a tomato and basil sauce. We couldn't wait. Luckily the afternoon flew by and before we knew it we were ready for a nice big healthy dinner. We pulled over at a roadside picnic spot and began to rustle up our new concoction. We had taken a liking to these roadside picnic spots, they were always nice places to stop and relax often separated from the road by a patch of well kept grass and a hedge, creating a secluded spot away from the noise of the road. We got the pasta on straight away; both starving and salivating at the meal we had ahead of us. It tasted as good, if not better than we had imagined. It was perfect, definitely hitting the spot. That was what we needed, we both agreed. Now all we had to do was cycle on another five kilometres to the 130 kilometre mark and begin looking for a place to camp, simple.

It wasn't simple. Those five kilometres had come and gone quickly with no yield of a place to camp. The problem was that we were on the N-67 a busy main road which was often raised up from the land around. There was no way to get down to the pastures that surrounded the road and no visible places to camp. We pedalled on, we had no option, although we were now getting a little bit worried that maybe our luck had caught up with us and this would be the night we would not find a place to camp. The light was fading now; we had a brief pep talk at the side of the road discussing options and decided that our best option would be to get off the road. So at the next junction we took the exit to the town of Vecqueville. Just like that we found a perfect spot. It was that simple. As we cycled off the N-67 we noticed a small path leading up from the roundabout into some trees. We followed the path and sure enough it eventually opened up into a field. Even better it was an empty field with short grass. Perfect for camping. It was sheltered from the wind and road by two lines of trees shielding us from view. It was our reward for having to deal with the busy roads.

The light was almost gone now so we quickly assembled the tent and jumped inside. Maybe tonight would be our night's sleep without any mosquitoes or slugs? All we could do was hope.

Danger of Death
Cycling Day 18
Vecqueville to Suippes

For once we had not endured a plague during the night. We woke up without any bites or any slugs, result! Although in the grand scheme of things this wasn't really an achievement it certainly felt like it was! It was a good way to start the day. We needed this pick me up because we woke up at the early hour of 6:54. We wanted to get on the road early and fast so that the N-67 would be as empty as possible. We really were not enjoying cycling on the N-roads; they were just too busy and not pleasant. The thought of cycling the first 90 kilometres of the day on them was really demoralizing. We were focused though; we would smash the 90 kilometres in the morning then have a nice lazy afternoon like we did during the first week of cycling.

We knew it was going to be hard but we were hoping that because the roads were going to be more major they would stay flatter. We were all packed up and on the bikes in under an hour. It was definitely one of our faster mornings. It had started positive, Tom and I just hoped that things would keep on getting better, and that there weren't too many trucks. Once the first 90 kilometres of likely stressful cycling were over we would be only a day from Belgium and a whole lot closer to our final destination. The anticipation that we were inside our final week now was building. We were so close. We had almost cycled around the whole of Europe. We just had to navigate the next 90 kilometres safely first, and then we could relax and be jubilant.

We started off hard. Our hands down in the drops, streamlined, with Tom's front wheel almost kissing my back wheel. Our legs were pushing over and over as they had done for the past 2000 odd kilometres. Only now we were really moving. We ignored the barrage of French car horns; we were immune to them now. We just rode, dawn broke and we still pushed. Only taking brief breaks for sweets and to take off layers as the sun rose and we were bathed in its warmth, yet again it was turning into a glorious summer day.

Before we knew it we had already passed through Saint Dizier, we grabbed a quick pain au chocolate and Iced Tea then pushed on towards Vitry-Le-François along the N4. It was long, it was straight, and it was filled with trucks. Need I go on? I definitely wouldn't put it up there with the best road for cycling. However today we were really pulling together as a team. We were motivating each other and we both knew the goal we had to achieve. Tom was focused to just keep pushing and as always I was knackered, so always keen to take a break. Together that meant we balanced each other out, taking the opportune amount of rest stops but still making great mileage.

The roads were long and hot, with the trucks kicking up great clouds of dirt, caking us in yet more filth. However I think our bodies had reached the peak amount of dirtiness, our skin was saturated with dirt so it felt like we didn't really get much more dirty. The realisation that we were probably not going to get a shower till we boarded the ferry had sunk in. Another four days without a shower.

The kilometres continued to tumble as we continued to pedal, that kind of is our cycling in a nutshell. We now had a mere hour more of pedalling till we would reach Chalons-Sur-Marne the end of the N44 and our beacon of hope the D977. We decided to have no breaks and to just gun it. We knew this stretch would not be pleasant to cycle so by just taking no breaks we could be done with it sooner and then go back to having a long lazy lunch and a lovely relaxed afternoon enjoying the battlefields of Northern France.

Finally when we felt our legs were about to fall off our junction arrived and we could take the exit onto the D977. Hallelujah! We had done it, cycled a very painful 93 kilometres by lunch. We tootled up the road a few hundred metres, till we found a delightful grassy knoll outside a caravan park. We rested our steeds against some trees, spread out the tarpaulin, lay down and relaxed. During those few minutes we didn't talk. We were battered, it was the heat of the day and we were both feeling beaten up by the N-roads. It wasn't that we were annoyed with each other we were just so tired and fatigued sometimes there is just nothing to say. We were probably slightly dehydrated, hungry and worn out. After a nice chill out under the trees we read our books, ate, drank, and soon peace and tranquillity was restored. We were recovered and the banter could begin again. There was no need to talk about these mood changes, they were a regular occurrence by now, we were used to them and we had found out how to deal with them. Just ignore them. Simple.

We were so happy that we had already cycled 93 kilometres, as the end was well and truly drawing near now. We would only have to cycle 130 kilometres a day in order to easily make the ferry. This meant we had only 35 or so kilometres left to cycle today. This afternoon was going to be well and truly relaxed.

We ended up spending about two hours having lunch and a little siesta. Then we decided we had better cycle on a bit to try and find a shop to get some food for dinner. This was typical us, always thinking about where the next meal would come from. However we struck luck when we arrived in the town of Suippes. Not only did they have a supermarket but it was our favourite little German supermarket, Lidl. Cue the second lunch. We now had just 10 kilometres left to cycle so thought we should stock up, and stock up we did. Many litres of Iced Tea were drunk, also many yogurts and Tom feasted on his favourite 'Crunch' chocolate bars. Not the most balanced meal but our Iced Tea did contain lemon. We just needed calories so took the view it didn't really matter what we ate just how much of it we could eat.

The town of Suippes seemed quite quiet, few people were about and it was all very sleepy. However it does border onto the 'Camp De Suippes' as we cycled along the D977 every few hundred metres on our right there would be another rusting red sign reading, "Keep out Camp de Suippes Danger of Death", well it read that but in French.

It was slightly unnerving cycling past it, especially when it seemed some of the signs had bullet holes in them. However we had come upon a slight problem. The road was totally flat. Now initially I agree that does not seem like much of a problem, far from it in fact, you may just be thinking that I think everything we face is a problem. Well the problem we had was that we were now looking for a place to set up our tent. Now as the area was completely flat there were no undulations for us to hide our tent behind. It was farmland so there was also no trees, it was just kilometre after kilometre of the same, oh and the odd war memorial.

Finally after long surpassing our daily goal we saw a cluster of trees in the distance. They looked ideal. We pedalled up to them and found a lovely spot out of view from the road. Another day camping in paradise. Well that was until Tom went to relieve himself and take a look inside the cluster of trees that seemed to be encircling a hidden area in the middle. He came back running suggesting we assemble the tent quickly. BEES! Yes, it was a bee farm. Thousands of the stinging buggers were living just a few metres from our tent and immediately I recognised what was crawling on my leg. Oh no not again, I thought to myself. Someone somewhere must be finding this all absolutely hilarious we thought, we settled in for yet another night being plagued by Mother Nature.

Belgium!
Cycling Day 19
Suippes to Couvin

We woke feeling good. We had managed to avoid the bees and evade being stung. Wahoo! Today there would be no N-roads; instead it would be a sedate cycle along the relaxing D-roads into country number six, Belgium. Our aim for today was to camp just the other side of the border, inside Belgium. We would then have two more proper cycling days before the final day, which would be a short pedal to the ferry.

It was music to our ears when we realised this. Almost three weeks of constant cycling every day had really taken it out of us. We were feeling thoroughly fatigued now. We were still enjoying the cycling but we felt pretty broken. Our muscles, despite having been in training for the past three weeks, were waning. There was no way we would be able to manage a 180 kilometre day now; luckily we didn't have to. Just 120 kilometres would do it for today and we both knew that would be enough. The fatigue was more of a mental state. The constant ups and downs, the stress of busy roads, the lack of sleep and the unrelenting need to keep on pedalling. Everything just built up on top of one another. So although we were enjoying it and having the time of our lives, we were suddenly realising, so close to the end, how mammoth the undertaking was.

It is precisely situations like this when you need mind over matter. That is why almost anyone can go on an adventure like this. If you have a good drive to succeed and complete your mission, then you will do it. You don't need hours and hours of training, it may help you a little at the beginning but it will rarely be a reason for you failing. If you have a drive to always push yourself and see new things, meet new people then you can do it and you will succeed.

We had a relaxed morning, cycling past another war memorial every 500 metres or so. It became apparent to us the shear scale of the numbers of deaths and how this region of France had been left totally desolated by it. After a couple of hours riding we reached the town of Rethel. It had been lovely and peaceful, almost no motor vehicles on the roads and just lots and lots of rolling hills. We still dislike the rolling hills but were growing slightly more accustomed to them. To be honest we were just looking forward to a day or so time when the roads would become completely flat. Once we arrived in Rethel we stopped for a 'well deserved' (as they always are) mid-morning breakfast. We also loaded up our supplies for the approaching lunch.

When it was time to leave Rethel that also meant it was time to change onto the last pre-loaded route on the GPS, from Rethel to Rotterdam. This meant we now had exactly 316 kilometres left to cycle. The end was finally approaching and the moment we had envisaged all those months ago was finally drawing closer. We had almost done it; just 316 kilometres and we would have cycled around Europe and have covered just over 3000 kilometres.

We were beginning to feel ever more nostalgic about the experiences we had endured through our adventure. The ups as well as the downs were both equally good to look back over. Then we could remind ourselves that it wasn't over just yet and no doubt we would still have a lot more experiences, most probably things going wrong knowing us.

The afternoon was as hot as ever. There was sunshine as usual and occasionally the odd cloud. We stopped for lunch at a roadside picnic spot, and dined on our lunchtime staple, chicken cous cous for me, tinned ravioli for Tom, both of us washing it down with copious amounts of lemon Iced Tea. We could relax. We were certain to make the ferry now, the one we had booked all those months ago. We only had to do about 120 kilometres so we could afford to chill. Have a long lunch, some nice stops off in the afternoon. It finally gave us a chance to properly enjoy and submerse ourselves in what was around us. We enjoyed this, it's all well and good pushing big miles and covering vast distances but we were really relishing being ahead of schedule. It gave us the opportunities we wouldn't otherwise be able to do. It reminded us of the previous summer when we had cycled to Paris. We had only done around 120 kilometre days during that and we had loads of fun. Maybe we were finally realising that this was our preferred distance. Although we loved the satisfaction of having long days in the saddle as you get a real sense of progress when you cover big distances. When you just have shorter days covering less distance you gain a real sense of meaning. Striking the balance between the two is a fine line and I think we had finally found ours at about 120 kilometres a day. However, saying that, doing longer days interspersed with shorter days worked well for us. I guess we learned you just have to take each day as it comes.

Soon the rolling hills began to roll less and the roads became longer and flatter. We knew we were nearing Belgium. We finally approached the border town of Rocroi and more importantly its Carrefour supermarket. Rocroi was a town unlike any we had cycled through before. We realised this as we approached, when I was perplexed by what I was seeing on the map. It appeared the town was in the shape of a star. When we went to inspect, it turned out that was a fortified town, each layer of the star being another wall. It was very impressive and we were contented with the fact that it appeared to have managed to survive two world wars without serious destruction.

Finally we made it to Belgium. If it wasn't for the line on the map we would have been none the wiser because everyone still spoke French, the signs we still all in French and it certainly looked very French. This was a first for us, often when we had crossed borders there was suddenly a stark change. Not with Belgium though, it felt very French, which in a way comforted us, we were used to France and we liked it. Once we arrived in country number six though the light was fading, we both knew it was time to find somewhere to sleep.

Fortunately this did not take long at all. We had arrived in an area of Belgium that was covered in forest. This gave us a huge number of possible camping spots. We eventually found one that seemed pretty perfect. It was totally out of view from the road, even though it was only about 40 metres away from it. We were enclosed from all sides in a forest. We both joked how now it was time to cue the axe wielding, murdering psychopath. This is not a reflection on the Belgians, rather the very horror film-esque set-up and surroundings of our camp.

We were reassured by the fact that no one would want to murder us. This was because of many reasons, one we didn't have anything worth stealing but mainly we were so smelly and dirty. I'm pretty sure our smell killed everything in about a thirty metre vicinity. This is what we needed to fight off the mosquitoes we thought, an overwhelming power of stench. The trees providing lots of cover made it dark very fast so we settled in for quite an early night. Tomorrow we will hit our next major cities of Charleroi and Brussels; there ain't no rest for the wicked.

A Country in a Day
Cycling Day 20
Couvin to Mechelen

We rose bright and early with the dawn chorus. An axe-wielding psychopath had not murdered us. Hooray! It was 6:45am but we were keen to get going. We wanted today to be our last biggish day. Our aim was to hit Charleroi mid-morning, Brussels mid-afternoon and then find somewhere to camp before we hit Antwerp. That would leave us with 100 kilometres the following day and then about 50 kilometres for the final day. Yes, the final day, we were getting tantalisingly close now.

It had been a good while since we had cycled through any major cities, our last one was Geneva and we went through that on a Sunday so that was not the busiest city. We therefore had a sneaky suspicion that Belgium was going to surprise us and be a lot more busy. We weren't keen of all the hustle and bustle, however we hoped it would provide a nice change of rhythm to our cycling. Also we would be seeing a capital city today so no doubt there would be a lot to see and do once we got there. Even if we weren't able to do much because we had two heavily laden bikes and were looking like scantily lycra-clad hobos.

From today everything was downhill, not literally although that would have been amazing, the days would get shorter, the cycling would get easier, the roads would get flatter, cycling would get more popular. That last point we were looking forward to, we were heading to the cycling capitals of the world, countries renowned for their brilliant cycle networks. We couldn't wait to test them out and meet more cyclists. We had met our fair share so far. We would probably average seeing one cycle-tourist a day and it always promoted a feeling of serendipity. Even if words weren't exchanged because we were travelling in opposite directions there was an understanding. You both knew that the other person was going through similar experiences to you, they were living the ups and downs, and they had also chosen the simple mode of transport to travel by. You were both seeing the world from similar perspectives and were exposed to the experiences the world had to throw at you. All these and many more are conveyed by a simple gesture of a wave, a smile or even a nod. In a way it is reassuring to know that there are people as crazy as you and that maybe for a moment you can kid yourself that the way you are travelling is the norm.

We had the bikes back up to the road in under an hour and were ready to start pedalling. As luck would have it the first ten kilometres were in fact all downhill. That made for a fun, fast and very cold morning. The sun was barely up and we hadn't had time to work up a sweat, so costing down, those first ten kilometres were nippy to say the least. Just like that we had almost done a tenth of today's mileage in about 20 minutes. If only the whole day was this easy we thought. We decided to stop after 20 minutes because we had made it to a Carrefour supermarket in the town of Couvin and were keen to load up on food for the day.

Tom took the first trip into the supermarket to scope out what produce they had whilst I guarded the bikes. Whilst he was inside a lovely old Belgian man approached me, the first Belgian we had actually met on this trip. He began to talk to me in French. Fortunately the previous three weeks had meant that our French was significantly better than it was at the beginning, almost back to our GCSE standard, although that was far from fluent. However I was still able to have a conversation with this man despite him not speaking a word of English. I explained what we were doing, where we had been and come from how long it had taken us, all the usual things we had to explain really. He then told me how he had cycled to Lourdes in France a couple of years ago, which I was very surprised at because this small-framed man had a cane and looked like he would have gone flying in the smallest of gusts of wind.

Couvin had turned out to be a fantastic stop and a wonderful way to start Belgium. Once I went inside the supermarket I found a whole isle of freshly baked pastries and thought I had gone to heaven. Tom had come out a few minutes previously and informed me that there wasn't a great selection of food. Had we entered different shops? When I came out with all my fresh baguettes, pains au chocolates, and of course Iced Tea he looked on in awe. After describing to him the locations of all of my finds Tom went in for a second bite at the cherry and came out with stocks of food. We carried on chatting with the old man for a while, before we realised we had been resting for over an hour and had only turned our pedals about 10 times so far today. We bid farewell and pushed onwards further into Belgium.

The roads had definitely flattened out a lot by now; this was also accompanied by the realisation that Belgian drivers are fantastic. They constantly gave us huge amounts of space, definitely some of the most considerate drivers we had met so far. However with every yin there is a yang. Unfortunately the yang in our case was the surface of the roads. Now if you think the state of potholes in the UK is bad. Please picture in your mind the most pot-holed road you know. Now multiply the number of potholes and the degradation of the road surface by about ten and you will arrive at the surface of a *good* Belgian road. I am not kidding. These were the worst roads Tom and I had seen in our lives. On the good stretches, on bigger roads, there was no asphalt, instead large cracked slabs of concrete made up the road surface, these were very poorly put together and obviously never maintained. There were regularly gaps of 15 centimetres in-between each slab. So that meant every 15 metres or so we would have an almighty bang as our wheels passed over another huge gap. Lord knows how our wheels didn't buckle under the constant barrage of knocks and bumps. We somehow didn't even puncture, although we had managed nearly 3000 kilometres without a puncture between us and we weren't going to start getting them now.

In the future we will think long and hard before complaining about the state of a British road. They are like pristine marble surfaces compared to Belgium. Another thing we found odd about Belgium's road network was that when there was no bike lane it was fine to be in the road.

However when there were bicycle lanes they were often on the pavement. This would mean cycling up and down curbs, over man-hole covers and over all the pavement pot-holes. We could not be bothered with this. We were like rivers flowing down a mountain, we would take the path of least resistance and if that meant not using the cycle lanes then that was our option. In the UK it is perfectly fine not to use the cycle lanes if they are there, so we assumed this would be the same in Belgium. It is not. Well it might be, but not according to the drivers we encountered. Everything is fine and dandy when there is no cycle lane, however when one becomes available boy do the drivers like to get on their horns and let you know about it.

Despite the terrible roads we managed to stay on target and we cycled through Charleroi mid-morning. We had long left the lovely forests of the south and had been cycling through industrial built up areas all morning. So far Belgium wasn't what we had been expecting. It seemed quite run down and depleted. Signs were battered, buildings eroding away, the huge holes in the road surface; we got the feeling that there was a lack of care. However one thing that was sure to brighten our moods was the weather. For yet another consecutive day the sun had come out in full force and we were loving it. It wasn't as hot as the south of France but it was perfect conditions for cycling, there was very little wind and we were enjoying pedalling towards Brussels.

We stopped for lunch at our regular, Aldi, this turned out to be one of the most well stocked Aldis of the trip so far. Not only did they have all the regular items we loved, including Iced Tea, they also had tins of baked beans. It had been so long since we had seen a tin of baked beans in a supermarket. It seems a bit of an anti-climax but it gave us immense pleasure seeing a food we would buy normally in a supermarket. It was a food we had longed for a long time. High in carbohydrate, protein, and tastiness, we had found our sustenance for the rest of the day. Although they were no comparison to Heinz they were not too bad and to us they tasted like success. It wasn't just the beans though that impressed us. I managed to find some socks. Yes you read that right, socks. I had been pedalling in the same pair since before I had the slug in my shoe; they were yellowing and not the nicest. So I was ecstatic at purchasing a pair of 'Sports Socks', for the princely sum of 1€. This afternoon my feet would be in comfort. Tom nursed himself into another chocolate coma by eating four huge bars of Belgian chocolate. We ate for about an hour, until the women who were working inside the shop motioned for us to leave.

We thought they were a bit mean because we weren't hurting anyone by eating our food outside the shop nor were we in anyone's way. Maybe it was our smell putting off customers! Luckily we were finished and both keen to keep on pedalling. We were only about 10 kilometres outside of Brussels now.

Those kilometres went fast; we were fuelled on beans, new socks and flat roads. We decided to go for our normal approach of discovering cities. Just go for a pedal. If we see things of interest, pedal towards them. It had worked brilliantly for us so far and we had no reason to doubt it working for us now. It was fantastic. We spent a good couple of hours pedalling the streets. Venturing down alleyways, across grand quadrangles, past churches, monuments and palaces. It was all very grand and really allowed us to immerse ourselves into the city. We finally took a break outside the impressive Law Courts of Brussels. They are the most important law courts in the whole of Belgium, situated in a grand palace designed by the architect Joseph Poelaert. It was actually the biggest building constructed in the 19th century. We sat and relaxed on a nearby wall, our backs to the law courts, overlooking the rest of Brussels spreading out below us. One large concrete building caught our eye. Not for its magnificence, quite the contrary, it looked appalling. It was your classic 1950s degrading concrete tower block. Rather comically on its roof someone had positioned large letters spelling out 'HOLLYWOOD', talk about optimism.

We chilled there for quite a while, taking in the views and relaxing. We knew we would easily make it out of Brussels and find a place to camp, so were not at all in a rush to move on. Instead we thought we would take in our final capital city of the trip.

Eventually the time came when we really had to move on. It was late afternoon and we wanted to avoid the probable rush hour. We began to slowly meander our way back across the city to our route. So we would be finally back on track. The meandering involved more small side streets and large churches, like the Eglise Royale Saint-Marie. I was being all the while careful to make sure my wheels did not become caught in the tram tracks. I did not want a re-creation of the Nice incident. Fortunately we made it out of the city unscathed.

We were however not rewarded with vast forests and farms, instead sprawling industrial madness. It just went on and on. Huge factories, large warehouses, it was worse than Trafford Park near where we rowed in Salford. It was unrelenting; after we had been pedalling for a good hour we had the decision to have a break. There was just nowhere to camp. Would this be it? Would this be our downfall? It was one of our last nights of the trip and the first not to yield a place to sleep. We decided to do the thing we knew best, pull over at a Lidl and get some food. We needed something to keep us going otherwise soon, no doubt, our tempers would stretch thin. The best option would be to pull over, eat and drink a little, Iced Tea of course. This would allow us to regroup so we could overcome our problem. We had taken this decision so many times before, by now it was sub-conscious. It worked well. We realised we only had one real option, to keep on pedalling. There was no need to worry about it because every extra kilometre today was one less tomorrow.

We continued down the N1 until we reached the outskirts of Mechelen. The road curved around to the left revealing a wood on the right. We were still in a heavily urbanised area so were not totally looking for a place to camp. We stopped nonetheless though because the Iced Tea had gone straight through us and we needed to empty the tanks. I trudged into the trees to get some cover. They then opened up into a full on forest. It was perfect! We would camp here. It looked almost totally undisturbed and there was dense coverage. We soon found what looked like a good spot to pitch the tent. However in the process we both got bitten on the legs. We thought nothing of it at the time. We were just happy to have a great place to camp. Once safely inside the tent though, the red marks began to grow. Our worst fears were soon realised, once again, mosquitoes! Luckily we had managed to trap them all outside the tent, we would just have to hope they were gone come morning time.

We Could Actually Do This
Cycling Day 21
Mechelen to Den Bommel

They were not gone. We woke to the ever increasing itchiness our bodies were experiencing. I had unknowingly been bitten the previous night on my left nipple, this had now swollen up to the size of a ping-pong ball, and it looked ridiculous. My huge puffy left nipple, what a sight for sore eyes, I tried not to care though because it was pretty funny. Tom especially found it hilarious, wanting to document the experience with photographs. After having plenty laughs at my woes we decided it was high time we get up and start pedalling, our last big day of cycling.

We were very hesitant to get out of the tent because we did not want to awaken the mosquitoes. The deadly biting nuisances of our trip. We had had enough of mosquitoes for the rest of our lives. They had tormented us for days across Europe. Obviously we were just their type. We eventually decided to pack everything up inside the tent then we could make a quick getaway and pack up the bikes back near the road, away from the mosquitoes. In theory this was a good plan. In practice not so much. You see mosquitoes are not stupid creatures, they sniffed out our plan and us, which wasn't hard given our very pungent smell. They bit and they stung, we itched, we cursed, and we swatted. Try as we might though we still got heavily bitten. Not to the same extent as we did at Saint-Maries-De-La-Mer but still pretty bad. These ones were huge as well, each bite swelled up to the size of a ping-pong ball making us, once again, look diseased.

Somehow we managed to pack everything up. However it took us a long time as we were constantly jumping around trying to evade the biters. After just over an hour we had successfully made it onto our saddles and were pedalling away from our final camping spot in Belgium. Tonight we would be close to Rotterdam and it would be our final night of camping wild. We knew today would be the last of a lot of things and that is why we shrugged off our copious amounts of bites. They were all part of the experience. The bites partly summed up our journey and therefore in a way it felt right and fitting to be bitten to shreds when we were almost at the end. We were happy and content, today would be the last full day of cycle touring on our adventure. After today we would begin to enter normality once again. It was an odd feeling as we had both, over the month, become accustomed to this way of life. We enjoyed the simplicity of life on the road. It was never boring, it was sustainable and most of all it was a different way to see the world. We had just 100 kilometres left of this so we would have to take it nice and easy to savour the feelings.

We weren't too far from Antwerp by now and our aim was to make it there by breakfast. Then we could push on into the Netherlands for lunch. That was our plan. One of the final plans we would have to make. Everything was all falling into place now. Tomorrow the ferry would predict our day. The one we had booked all those months ago, yet somehow we would make it and arrive on time.

Having breakfast in Antwerp was nice. It felt the entire city was still asleep; with it being a Saturday that could have been true. We managed to find a small Aldi and purchased a 'healthy' breakfast of stroopwafels and Iced Tea. Whilst eating our breakfast we continued to marvel at the ever-increasing popularity of cycling. There were increasingly fewer cars and increasingly more bicycles the further we cycled. It was fantastic. It was obvious the Belgian government had invested a lot of money into cycling infrastructure, if only our own government would follow suit we thought. We were now out of the French speaking part of Belgium, fortunately everyone seemed to speak fantastic English and not only that everyone was lovely. There was not one person we met or spoke to whom did not have a smile on their face. Despite today's weather being the worst it had been on the trip so far, there was heavy cloud cover and only a little blue sky, our spirits were high. Although this weather was hard to deal with when we had been treated to nearly a month of sunshine; we thought we had better get used to it. Before we knew it we would be back in Manchester, a city known for its *fantastic* summer weather.

We began the final push towards The Netherlands, our seventh country. We just got happier and happier. Everything was, finally, falling into place. The roads were increasing in quality, the number of cyclists was increasing, and even the sun was coming out now. We managed to cycle the whole way to The Netherlands on cycle paths. These were not simple sections on a road marked by a small smear of paint. These were purpose built smooth asphalt roads for cycling. Our poor bikes had been knocked and bumped around Europe. Now they were getting their reward for transporting us all this way and not giving in. They had not received a single puncture. Although they had suffered broken brakes, a bent wheel, shredded bar tape, that was all superficial and no matter what they just kept on rolling. They had carried us come rain or shine, minus the rain. Our saddles had not given us saddle sores, our pedals had not hurt our feet and our chains had not broken. For all that we were grateful. We were beginning to appreciate the smaller things in the trip. How we had not been lost, except on the second day when we had ended up on the motorway in Spain.

Today was turning into one of the best days of the trip. The cycling was easy; there were absolutely NO hills. We were now at an elevation of 0 metres above sea level. Boy had we come a long way since the 2108 metres on the top of the Col du Mont Cenis. We had cycled nearly 3000 kilometres and we were still going. Indeed we probably would continue to keep on going but that promise of the bed and a shower on the Ferry held us on course and to our target. We had also heard that we had now raised £3000 for the MS Society and money was still coming in. This we were over the moon about, we had raised a pound a kilometre and for such a good cause. Not only had we had fun but we were content that the pain and suffering which we had experienced had benefitted someone else somewhere. We realised that it is easy for someone to just check our page and not donate, why should they it seems everyone nowadays is doing an event for a good cause and trying to raise money. However to those people that did donate, they not only helped the cause but they also helped propel us. It didn't take much, we were happy with any donation, big or small, it just was reassuring that people were taking time out to invest in what we were doing and try and help us achieve the goals we set out to achieve. So to everyone that donated I must say a huge thank you as we would not have got this far without you spurring us on.

I say 'this far', although we haven't even finished. We had made it to The Netherlands and we now knew that it was all downhill from there, literally. We had a mere 50 kilometres left to cycle and then we would be at the Europoort ferry terminal just outside Rotterdam. 50 kilometres, that's nothing, we thought to ourselves. Then finally we would be able to stop pedalling.

Once we entered The Netherlands there was yet again a distinct change. The roads were, by a country mile, the best we had ever experienced. The complete opposite end of the scale to the shameful Belgian ones, we didn't even ride on any of the cobbled roads I imagine they would have been much more worse. The Dutch road network though was amazing; we instantly fell in love with it. I know that sounds sad, but after those Belgian roads it felt like a godsend. Next to the main roads were wide separate roads just for cycles, only even better than the ones we had experienced in the latter stages of Belgium. It seemed bicycle touring was the national sport as well, every five minutes or so another group would go by, their bikes significantly more loaded than ours. Every tourer we saw had at least five panniers, in comparison to our measly two each. We couldn't really comprehend what they might have been carrying but had fun posing ridiculous guesses as to what they might be concealing.

We took regular breaks throughout the afternoon, we weren't travelling fast now, and there was no need. So our thinking was, 'Why not just take a break?' So we had begun to take them every half an hour. This was a lesson in how to cycle-tour. Ultimate relaxation! We made a mental note for next time. It is definitely a good idea to lower our expectations, go slower, see more, and not kill ourselves. It seemed quite obvious but we had negated to do this properly until our last day of riding. Well if you could call it our last day of riding, with the amount of breaks we were taking now it felt more like a sedate holiday than a mammoth 3000 kilometre cycle around Europe.

Despite all the relaxing somehow we still felt tired. Nearly a month on the road and over three weeks cycling had totally worn us out; we were eager to finish. I think this was due to the fact that in our minds we had been building ourselves for this moment. Suddenly the shackles of the task had been removed; our focus had ended. This meant our minds were privy to the other things going on, things that earlier in the trip we just had to ignore and bare our teeth through. We were realising other things. Our moods were significantly improved without the incessant drive; there was simply no pressure any more. All our worries had been swept away, with every pedal stroke we became freer, and we became more close to finally clutching our goal. We would overcome the doubters and any doubts in our minds. Our sweat dripping faces had been replaced with content smiles. Our bodies bore the scars, the bites, the salt marks and the dirt, which told our story. The sheer scale of what we were about to accomplish was almost sinking in. We were 40 kilometres away from Rotterdam; if we wanted we could probably catch today's ferry.

We wouldn't though; we wanted to prolong this feeling. This cycle tour had turned into something special. It was probably the biggest thing either of us had accomplished so far in our lives; we had raised a huge amount of money and suffered a lot to do it. However that made our victory taste all that sweeter. Yes things had gone wrong, but in the grand scheme of things we would remember how we overcame those difficulties. What doesn't kill you only serves to make you stronger. Deep down we knew that and we were grateful of the trials we had experienced. We felt wizened, to the life of Europe and to life in a tent for a month. It can get pretty smelly.

We carried on cycling off and on for the whole afternoon, stopping regularly in towns and villages, drinking Iced Tea and buying food. It was great. Eventually we found a superb camp spot. However it was probably one of our most audacious ones yet. We camped off the small cycling path that ran parallel to the motorway. We were in full view of everyone but that didn't matter. We knew nothing would happen. You can trust more people than you think, a month on the road had certainly taught us that. If it's smuggling you through border tunnels or stopping to give you some food, people will always show superb generosity, especially if you are on a bicycle.

Our camping spot was idyllic, despite being next to a motorway. We were situated on a small island in the middle of the Hollands Diep river; just a stone's throw from

Rotterdam. Tomorrow all we would have to do is cycle 30 kilometres by 7:00pm, I think a much needed lie-in is in order.

Next Stop, Home
Cycling Day 22
Den Bommel to Rotterdam

We slept in till ten o'clock, definitely our record for a tent. We felt amazing. Today was the day. Today we would do it. Today we would complete our mission. More importantly tonight we would sleep in a mediocre bed and have an un-powerful shower. We were over the moon. We didn't care about how poor the facilities would probably be on the ferry because we would get luxuries we could only dream of after a month in the tent. Almost anything would be an upgrade. It's not that we didn't enjoy the tent; in fact we loved it. We just couldn't wait for the change of scenery and a bed would do that for us. Once again we would appreciate the little things, running water, soap, but most importantly beds.

All this was less than thirty kilometres away, just over and hour. Then we would be finished. There would be no finishing line, no welcome party either, but this didn't bother us. We didn't need any of that. We had cycled around Europe. We had never taken a rest day. Let the partying begin.

We took our time packing down the tent. Both of us were grinning solidly from ear to ear. We were about to accomplish what we had planned to do all those months go. It felt like a momentous day, although in a nutshell all we had done was to keep on turning our pedals for extended periods of time, it was a lot more than that. We were completing our goals, succeeding; there is no greater feeling than that. Success was a mere thirty kilometres away and we could taste it. The roads were flat, the asphalt was smooth, there was no head wind, and everything it seemed was finally in our favour. Finally we were hitting a string of good luck; we would end this trip on a high.

We had one other thing to do today. That was to find an open supermarket to buy some celebratory drinks and some food. So when we had finally packed away the tent and all our stuff for the very last time we clipped into our pedals and pushed off towards completion.

We rode talking and fantasising about finally ending this huge journey we had embarked upon. The moment we had been dreaming about for months was finally upon us. We were both so glad it had come; that we were still together and still good friends through all we had been through. So many times I had heard of people embarking on huge expeditions in teams or duos with their friends and then part way through them falling out with each other. I was glad this hadn't happened with me and Tom. Don't get me wrong we did have small arguments but these were mostly due to one of us being in a bad mood, we both knew this and so both knew the arguments didn't mean anything. As they meant nothing they were soon forgotten and nothing more needed to be said. We had not once had a proper argument and for that I am overjoyed. It meant that we could finish how we both dreamt of finishing, as a team and as best friends.

With excitement filling the air we kept on sedately pedalling towards our goal. It was a dull day, one of the first we had experienced. Knowing our luck with the weather though and our amazingly good moods we were both certain that it would brighten up. It was a sleepy day. No one else was on the roads. This gave The Netherlands a very eerie feel. Even the motorway when we woke up was barely making a sound. Then it clicked. It was a Sunday. Suddenly we knew our odds of finding an open supermarket were significantly lowered. We knew all-to-well by now that mainland Europe on a Sunday is pretty much a no go. Nowhere would be open, our plan of buying some premium Dutch beer had gone down the drain. However we vowed not to fail. Instead we looked around on the map for nearby towns that would hopefully have an open supermarket. First we tried the town of Nieuw-Beijerland, yet it was to no avail. Not a single soul in the town seemed to be awake. We had no option but to carry on towards our goal.

We were then a little bit perplexed. The road just ended. There was no way to carry on. Instead the river Spui blocked our path. There was no bridge instead the road just disappeared. Then we saw it, the ferry. Well not the ferry but a ferry. It seemed we would have to get a ferry across this 30-metre stretch of water. Why wouldn't they just build a bridge? We were totally confused. However we still had to reach our destination and had no other alternative route so boarded the ferry for the shortest boat journey of our lives. Alongside us were about ten other cyclists, ranging from elderly women on their Dutch strollers to lycra-clad, shaved-legged, middle-aged men on their carbon frames –I'm sure you know the type. The journey went without incident and 30 seconds later, after paying the princely sum of about 70 cents, we were delivered on the other side. The ferry then picked up more passengers and began its way back to the other shore. We just stood there and laughed, it just seemed so strange. The ferry just went 30 metres forwards and backwards all day long. We assumed they must have been using the money and saving up to buy a bridge as the current system seemed so odd.

By now we were mightily hungry; those 10 or so kilometres had really worked up our appetites. Also we were still in search of some celebratory alcohol for the ferry. We made the decision to once again set off in the wrong direction in search of an open supermarket. We were heading towards the town of Spijkenisse. It looked quite large on the GPS map so we were hopeful. However once we arrived we realised that like the town of Nieuw-Beijerland no one was awake. It was like being in a ghost town, we drifted through the windy streets, meandering our way across the town. Not a single shop was open, not a single soul was awake. It was now approaching noon and we still hadn't found anywhere! No food and no drink. Could it be that on the final day of our journey would be the first day we would have to go thirsty and hungry?

We were beginning to tire; the unrelenting search for an open supermarket was exhausting. We were bored of getting lost in town centres so decided to make our way back to the route and move ever closer towards the ferry terminal at Rotterdam. One thing we were not tired of though were the fantastic cycle paths. They were amazing. Incredibly smooth, pothole-less, asphalt. If only the roads had been this good the whole way round, the cycle would have been a whole lot more pleasant. However I don't know if it would have been better. Cycling on good roads for 3000 kilometres may have got a tad monotonous. We would not had had the same experience of perils on the roads, huge trucks and motorways in Spain, almost getting run over by a metro in Nice, the horrible potholes of Belgium. Yes these were all horrible things at the time. Some of which I still bear the scars to, most notably the large scar on my left knee which serves as a memento of that day in Nice. It was these events though which gave us exciting tales to tell, or so we hoped, they made our journey what it was. They taught us lessons about a whole range of things. For that reason I am grateful of everything that happened on our trip and that the roads weren't nice the whole way round.

On that note we were over the moon to be finishing the cycle on the best roads we had cycled on. I am not sure if our crotches could have taken another few hundred kilometres of those Belgian potholes. The sun was now shining and we had a mere five kilometres to cycle to the end. Five kilometres! Out of 3000! We had almost done it. We could taste the sea air, feel our beds awaiting us on the ferry, and we could almost see the finishing line.

Just before we began our final push though we spied an open shop! Albeit a petrol station, this would be our last purchase on mainland Europe we didn't really care that the food was over priced. We feasted on sandwiches and crisps, hardly a victory meal but we agreed that would come later on the ferry. We may have been eating a normal bag of crisps and some peculiar looking sandwiches but they tasted like success. We had pushed so hard for so long just for this feeling, this euphoria, this rush. It had been worth it. We were on top of the world, although we may not have looked it. To anyone looking we were just two unshaven, dirty, smelly, teenage boys possibly looking a bit too over pleased at their distinctly mediocre lunches.

After our final lunch stop of the cycle we hopped onto our bikes for the final push to the ferry. They were quick kilometres as well. The odometer on the GPS was counting down. With every pedal stroke we were closer and closer to achieving our goal. Our grins were from ear to ear. We just wanted to reach the ferry terminal, sit down and toast to our achievement. Despite cycling at 30kph we still managed to be overtaken by a couple of Dutch cyclists. They shouted in characteristically Dutch accents, "Where you guys from?"

"Manchester!" We replied.

"Super nice", was the response we got back and then they were gone. That was the extent of our welcoming party. It didn't bother us, we had started it out alone and we would finish it alone.

As we passed under the P&O signage for Hull the end point finally came into view on the tiny screen of the GPS. It was deserted all around us. Obviously no one else wanted to show up five hours before the due departure of the ferry. We pedalled, following the little red arrow on the GPS to the end. We rounded the corner and saw it. It stood magnificently in front of us. The finish line. Our final transportation. The Pride of Rotterdam ferry. The odometer clicked over one final time and the GPS confirmed we had reached the end of our route.

Our adventure was over. The ordeal of the past few weeks, the stresses, the pains all went away. Just like that with a few breaths we could finally relax. It was an odd sensation as the final kilometre had been no different to any other that we had cycled. Yet it seemed to give us so many more rewards. In the shadow of the huge ferry we finally dismounted our bikes. We embraced each other like long lost brothers. We had done this as a team. We had done this together. We had not fallen out. We both stank, we both desperately needed showers, we had both shared the same experiences. However we would no doubt both take different thoughts home with us. One thing we were both sure of though was that Rotterdam would not be the end. The past month had taught us a lot about teamwork and working together, one thing we now knew was that we work well as a team. We will continue to work well as a team and go on many more adventures together, possibly even longer than this one.

Acknowledgements

Tom and I had a tough month cycling around Europe however if it wasn't for the support we received along the way it would have been much harder. Whether it was people stopping to give us some fruit, giving us lifts through tunnels, or just lifting our spirits by having a nice conversation. People never ceased to propel us on our journey and lift our spirits. It is these interactions which are the fondest to look back upon and make both of us want to continue going on more adventures and meet new people.

We also received, if not more, support from home though and it was this which also propelled us around Europe. My parents, Sue and Graham, and brother, Scott, were updating our website letting other people know of our progress. They also helped us out by driving us down to the ferry and forming a great welcome party when I finally cycled up to my front door. Also with supportive texts and calls throughout our journey they were always behind us. Tom's parents, Duncan and Gill, and sister, Lucy, were also really helpful in sending supportive messages and organising yet more sponsorship for the MS Society.

I would also like to thank everybody that donated money to the MS Society via our Internet page, (justgiving.com/europe-cycle) it really means a lot and I have seen that money we raised has directly made a big difference to the lives of MS sufferers. That is why I am donating £1 from the sale of every book to the MS Society so that our cycle can have a prolonged effect and hopefully raise a lot more money. So to everybody that donated: Rose Woollard, Alice Iball, Neil Sheldon, Rachel Sharkey, Tracey Donnelly, Tom's Grandparents, Claire Hulme, Anna Tatton, Susan Dawson, Rosemary Morgan, Helen Light, Janet Hancock, Ramzi Ajjan, Gail Douglas, Lynne and Justin Woolley, Christopher Lock, Elizabeth Farthing, Margaret Williams, David Owens, Thomas Fleming, Peter Knapp, Amy Russell, Chris Inglehearn, Carolyn Czoski-Murray, Fiona Henderson, Joanna Zakrzewska, Yvonne Flanagan, Terence Lee, Nick Phillips, Karena Heslop, Jenny Porrit, Gavin Giovannoni, Isabel Hanson, Edith, Chris Weir, Christopher and Carol Ray, Maya Buch and Prakash Manoharan, Mark Mon-Williams, Ann Walker, Anne Higgins and Geoff Iball, Maureen Twiddy, Jeremy Chataway, Michael and Jeanette Ruane, David Broadbent, The Stirling family, Tracey Farragher, Doug Brown, The Briggs family, The Davidson family, Trevor Pavitt, Alexa Ruppertsberg, Graham Stansfield, The Muir family, Christopher Mayer, Phillip Crawley, The Pankiws, Jenny A, Leon Smith, Mick and Sophie Joyce, Kelly Watson, Alison Bone, Louise Butler, Diane Mitchell, Aarun, John Wilkinson, Lucy Priestner, Anne Priestner, Alison Hill, Jeanette and Ged, Charlotte Burt, Brian Handley, Phil and Charlotte Platt, Morspan Construction, The Higton family, David Keane, Maria Morasso, Tim Smith, Jawad Khawaja, Annabel, David Miller, Meniru family, Judith Adams, Karen Inns, Nicola Kitching, Liz and Rod Harrington, Amanda Gilbert, Patricia Gaskell, Elizabeth Foster, Michael Rusted, Steve Jones, James Duffy, Martin McKibbin, Frances Lucibello, Mike Davies, Bob and Pam Davies, Mark Priestner, Ralph Odell, Monty Duggal, Simon McCormick, and Sandrina Parry-Bargiacchi.

Also I would like to thank any future donations made to our just giving page. Finally thank you to you for purchasing this book as every little helps to make the world a better place.

Kit List

Tom and I both thoroughly enjoyed our time on the road and it was at times made significantly easier by the kit we took along with us. The type of equipment you take with you on cycle-tour really depends on *you*. I think it is important in first understanding what you are trying to attempt with your cycle-tour and then finding the gear that may help you achieve that goal. With that in mind this list is by no means exhaustive it is simply a congregation of items which we found to be useful during our month cycling. Everyone will have their own personal preference but these items worked for us so if you are thinking of attempting something similar I'd recommend checking out these items. If you are looking for more advice on cycle-touring or have any questions or comments about this book please do feel free to contact me via my blog; alexscycle.org

Bike – Possibly the most important piece of kit, make sure you are comfortable riding it and get it serviced every few thousand kilometres. I rode a Giant Defy 2 and Tom road a Specialized Secteur.

Pedals – Choosing a pair of clipless pedals and shoes will improve your efficiency on the bike. You can get touring-specific shoes which allow you to easily walk about a campsite when off the bike.

Ortlieb Rear Roller Panniers – great capacity and very waterproof, they also proved to be slug-proof as well on a couple of occasions. We managed for the month with just two panniers each.

Bungee Cords – A necessity for attaching things to your bike, we used these all the time, as they are just so useful!

Tent – We opted for a two-man MSR Hubba Hubba, highly waterproof, portable and the right shade of green for blending in to your surroundings. In the future though I think I'll opt to have my own tent so that I can escape Tom's snoring.

Tarpaulin – A simple military tarpaulin we found very useful for covering our belongings and bikes while wild camping. They provide waterproof cover, and double up as a raincoat, picnic blanket or groundsheet for a tent. You can also just camp under them and do away with the tent. Great cheap piece of equipment and will always come in useful.

Sleeping Bag – We went for lightweight summer ones but obviously choose one that will suit the conditions you are expecting.

Sleeping Mat – We opted for Thermarest NeoAirs, I have never had any problems with mine and Tom has had his replaced since returning, his kept on deflating due to a faulty valve. A good nights sleep is important so you want to make sure you have a good mat.

Camping Stove – What stove you get depends on where you will be cycling and what fuel will be available. We used a Campingaz one that was reliable and we had no problems cooking up some tasty meals on it. Remember fuel and a cooking pot so that you can use it!

Spork – A multifunctional eating tool that saves weight on additional cutlery.

Dehydrated Meals – We took a couple of these to use as emergency rations. During the month away we only had to use one each, but if we hadn't had any then we would have gone very hungry. They're not always the nicest meals but its all calories at the end of the day.

Clothes – Depends how dirty you want to be to how much you take. We opted for a couple of pairs of cycling clothes and one 'off the bike' outfit. On reflection the cycling clothes became dirty within a day so we'll just stick to one pair of these in the future to save weight. You can always get more clothes on your journey if you need some. It's also probably a good idea to take a warmer jacket for evenings.

Cycling Gloves – Save your hands if you have a crash and provide extra warmth if you are travelling in colder areas.

Sunglasses

Helmet – Yeah you don't look cool but it could save your life so is worth wearing.

Dry-Bags – For storing equipment within your bags or panniers they make it easier to find things and keep things dry. Also if you fill one with clothes you can use it as a pillow.

Flip-Flops – These you can just clip to the outside of your bag or onto your bike with a carabiner. They mean you can air your feet after a days riding and also give you a pair of footwear for rest days.

Camera – You never know what you might see!

GPS – Definitely not for everyone but we found it really useful, especially when we had to re-navigate our way out of Spain not using motorways. We used a Garmin eTrex Vista HCx, although designed for walking it is perfect for cycle-touring, very reliable and not very expensive second hand!

Mobile Phone – And accompanying charger. iPhones are good but an old Nokia can last well over a week on a single charge.

Watch – We used ones with a heart rate monitor function so that we could measure how many calories we were burning. However on reflection one with an alarm would be more fitting for those early starts.

Passport – Although we only had to flash ours once despite going through eight countries it is always good to have. Also if you are travelling in Europe remember your EHIC card. It also might be a good idea to take out travel insurance but I'll leave that to you.

Money – It might be worth splitting your money up into different places in your panniers so you won't lose all of it should the worse happen.

Diary – I really recommend writing a diary during your travels as they provide great mementos to look back over.

Book – Or Kindle / eReader. These have superb battery lives now that they offer a much lighter and attractive alternative to carrying a whole library with you.

First Aid Kit – We just had a small one with a variety of plasters, bandages and medicines. You can often stock up on your journey so I wouldn't recommend taking a big one. I would recommend some strong mosquito spray though; not taking that was definitely an oversight.

Toiletries – A bar of soap / shampoo can do you for everything, even cleaning the cooking pot. Sun cream is very important for the first week or two. Deodorant to mask foul smells and earplugs if you are travelling with a snorer. Toothbrush, toothpaste, toilet roll, hand sanitizer, and a razor if you feel like shaving your legs. Travel towels are also very useful and lightweight. These items are mostly down to personal preference so take what you think you might use.

Bike Maintenance Kit – Very handy, although we didn't have much use for one you never know what might happen, a hand pump, with a couple of spare inner tubes are a good idea; I even took a spare folding tyre.

Paracord – A few metres wound up in the bottom of your bag, you never know when it will come in useful.

Duct Tape – Again a very useful commodity, not a whole roll but a small bit could help you out in that time of need.

Cycle Lights – For night time riding and for long tunnels. Head torches are also useful.

Water Bottles – We carried just under 2 litres in water bottles and then often had a bottle of Iced Tea tied to our pannier racks.

Bike Lock – This is personal preference, we took some small ones so that we could save weight. These consisted of a small Kryptonite D-lock with Kryptoflex cable, and a Kryptoflex cable with a padlock. We also tied these cables round our bags at night and had no trouble with any thefts.

A good friend – I think going on a trip like this with a good friend or friends makes it a whole lot more fun. An experience shared is an experience gained. I am so glad that I had Tom there to push me through the lows, so that we could enjoy the highs together. We will always be able to look back and reminisce over this trip together. Going on an adventure like this shows that you really know a person and lets you know whom your true friends are. So as we are only young we are sure that we will go on many more adventures together.